THE
NOIR
STYLE

THE
NOIR
STYLE

ALAIN SILVER &
JAMES URSINI

Additional material by
Robert Porfirio and Linda Brookover

Design by Bernard Schleifer

THE Overlook PRESS
WOODSTOCK • NEW YORK

First published in the United States in 1999 by
The Overlook Press, Peter Mayer Publishers, Inc.
Lewis Hollow Road
Woodstock, New York 12498

Catalog-in-Publication Data is available from the Library of Congress

Reginald Marsh
SMOKE HOUNDS, 1934, 36 x 30
egg tempera on masonite
Reprinted courtesy of the Collection of the Corcoran Gallery of Art, Washington, DC
Gift of Felicia Meyer Marsh
58.26

Edward Hopper
DRUG STORE, 1927, 29 x 40 1/8 in.
Oil on Canvas
Reprinted courtesy of the Museum of Fine Arts, Boston
Bequest of John T. Spaulding

Weegee
"Accident on Grand Central Station" and "He Is as he was left in the
Gutter (DOA on Arrival)" reprinted courtesy of Weegee/ICP/Liaison

Type formatting by Bernard Schleifer Company
Manufactured in Hong Kong
First Edition
1 3 5 7 9 8 6 4 2
ISBN 0-87951-722-0

ACKNOWLEDGMENTS

MOST OF THE ILLUSTRATIONS USED IN THIS BOOK CAME FROM THE AUTHORS' own collections. While we have endeavored to avoid duplicating images which appear in *Film Noir: An Encyclopedic Reference to the American Style*, many of the stills not used there but acquired in collaboration with Elizabeth Ward in preparation for that book now appear in *The Noir Style*.

Other stills from the classic period were kindly loaned to us by David Chierichetti, James Paris, Robert Porfirio, Janey Place and Lowell Peterson, Lee Sanders, and Robert E. Smith. The frame enlargements are from the Robert Porfirio Collection at Brigham Young University administered by James D'Arc. Some neo-noir stills were provided by Todd Erickson and the Robert Wise library of the Directors Guild of America. The stills are reproduced courtesy of Allied Artists, Allied Films, American Releasing, Columbia, Filmensa, Gramercy, MGM, Orion, Overseas, Paramount, RKO, Republic, Selznick, 20th Century-Fox, United Artists, Universal, and Warner Bros. Paintings are reproduced courtesy of The Museum of Fine Art, Boston, and The Corcoran Gallery of Art. The "Weegee" photographs are reproduced courtesy of Weege/ICP/Liaison Agency.

Most of the research for this volume is indistinguishable from that performed for our previous books and articles on film noir. A significant portion of that also overlaps with preparation of books on the work of Raymond Chandler and Robert Aldrich. For all that we are grateful to the staffs of the Margaret Herrick Library of the Academy of Motion Picture Arts and Sciences, the Theater Arts at UCLA, and the AFI Library. The idea for this volume was refined during conversations and correspondence with many others, most particularly Peggy Thompson and Saeko Usukawa (authors of *Hard-Boiled: Great Lines from Film Noir*); Jim Milio, Melissa Jo Peltier, and Mark Hufnail of MPH Productions; Paul Joyce at Lucida Productions; Robert Wise, Walter Hill, Andre de Toth, and Richard Schickel. To briefly recap the suggestions and support of others going back to 1974, we must thank again Janey Place, Lowell Peterson, Richard Thompson, and Tim Hunter; Elizabeth Ward and Carl Macek; David Bradley; Selise Eiseman; Mark Haggard and Bruce Kimmel; Linda Brookover; and India for her youthful perspective on what guns mean in movies.

CONTENTS

INTRODUCTION

The mood of tragedy is enhanced by a strong contrast of deep blacks and glaring whites—shadows and highlights. In drama we light for mood, we paint poems. Lighting with its ups and downs becomes a symphonic construction paralleling the dramatic sequences. —JOHN ALTON

In the world of film noir style becomes paramount; it is all that separates one from meaninglessness . . . critics have always been slow on the uptake when it comes to visual style. Like its protagonists, film noir is more interested in style than theme, whereas American critics have been traditionally more interested in theme than style. —PAUL SCHRADER

WHEN ENGLISH-LANGUAGE CRITICS BEGAN WRITING ABOUT FILM NOIR IN THE LATE 1960s, after the classic period of the cycle had already ended, the issue of style was secondary to the search for the defining characteristics of the movement. As Paul Schrader was quick to point out in "Notes on Film Noir," his seminal 1972 essay, "almost every critic has his own definition of film noir, and personal list of film titles and dates to back it up." Whether or not one agrees with Raymond Durgnat's assertion in his 1970 essay "The Family Tree of Film Noir" that "film noir is not a genre, as the Western and gangster film, and takes us into the realm of classification by motif and tone," almost all critical commentators would agree that style is a key element in understanding film noir.

In the first two chapters of their 1955 book *Panorama du Film Noir Amèricain* Raymond Borde and Ètienne Chaumeton discuss a definition of film noir and its sources. In their third chapter, "The War Years and the Formation of a Style," they are the first to associate Welles's *Citizen Kane*, Ford's *The Grapes of Wrath*, and even Preston Sturges's *Sullivan's Travels* with the emergence of a "Noir Style." Borde and Chaumeton deem the root of film noir style to be "in large measure 'anti-social'." Place and Peterson in their essay "Some Visual Motifs in Film Noir" call the same phenomenon "anti-traditional," specifically as opposed to the high-key convention which they deem "the dominant lighting technique which had evolved by the early Forties."

What all are reacting to is film noir's deviation from the conventional methods of Hollywood. Obviously nothing in the noir style, no individual scheme of lighting, framing, staging, cutting etc. is without some antecedent in some earlier film. But to suggest, as some more recent commentators have, that this invalidates the concept is to beg the question. By definition, style only emerges after it is consistently imposed on a body of work over time. Our purpose here is not to pinpoint when or where that style emerged but to survey its entire impact over film noir. It may be that the reader will conclude from our observations that Schrader is right when he maintains that "because film noir was first of all a style, because it worked out its conflicts visually rather than thematically, because it was aware of its own identity, it was able to create artistic solutions to sociological problems." Or it may be that the noir style will seem too ephemeral to permit such a broad statement.

From our perspective, who creates style is of secondary importance. Certainly the factors at work in the staging of any movie scene are not only multiform but are also subject to manipulations by diverse persons. It is the working method in the American film industry for one person to direct the motion picture. While today this may mean shaping the performances of the actors and supervising the work of all the other creative personnel, it is not our assertion that this was always or even mostly the case during what most agree is the classic period of film noir, the two decades from 1940 to 1960. Schrader, who believes that "style determines the theme in every film," looks not just to directors but to cinematographers and writers for the authorship of that style. "Perhaps the greatest master of noir," Schrader effuses, "was Hungarian-born John Alton, an expressionist cinematographer who could relight Times Square at noon if necessary. No cinematographer better adapted the old expressionist techniques to the new desire for realism."

Not being rooted in any filmmaker or filmmakers but in the general scope of film history and in the specific noir films themselves, the noir style stands on its own. While we agree with Durgnat and Schrader that film noir is a movement or cycle and not a genre, we do not contend that style determines the theme of every noir film or that the visual stylists are the sole creators of the noir cycle. Still, the self-consciousness of someone like Alton, who wrote about his techniques in a book entitled *Painting with Light*, can help one to understand the collective creative assumptions which contributed to the noir style and its evolution.

Although he photographed only a dozen or so noir films, Alton and other "mainstream" directors of photography like Nick Musuraca at RKO or John F. Seitz at Paramount helped to develop and sustain the visual homogeneity of film noir. Many commentators have written at length about the influences of German Expressionism and expatriate European filmmakers on noir. But in terms of pure technique, as he worked and wrote about his work in 1949, Alton understood the difference between application and innovation. He also knew that, as renowned cinematographer James Wong Howe would still assert twenty years later in 1969, "there are very few techniques being used that weren't used in the early silent days." In an era long before bluescreen and computer graphic effects, filmmakers could employ process photography, mattes, miniatures and the like. But preeminently cameramen like Seitz and Musuraca, Howe and Alton believed in the power of light. Alton illustrated this belief in *Painting with Light* at the end of his chapter on "Mystery Lighting":

> To realize the power of light and what it can do to the mind of the audience, visualize the following little scene:
>
> The room is dark. A strong streak of light sneaks in from the hall under the door. The sound of steps is heard. The shadows of two feet divide the light streak. A brief silence follows. There is suspense in the air. Who is it? What is going to happen? Is he going to ring the bell? Or just insert a key and try to come in? Another heavier shadow appears and blocks the light entirely. A dim hissing sound is heard, and as the shadow leaves, we see in the dim light a paper slip onto the carpet. The steps are heard again… This time they leave. A strong light appears once more and illuminates the note on the floor. We read it as the steps fade out in the distance.
>
> "It is ten o'clock. Please turn off your radio. The Manager."

A more graphic illustration of Alton's stylistic outlook is the often-reproduced image from the end of *The Big Combo* (1955). While the two figures are not identifiable from this shot, the viewer knows that they are Susan Lowell (Jean Wallace) and Leonard Diamond (Cornel Wilde). The viewer also knows that Diamond, a police detective, has been obsessively amorous of Susan Lowell, the moll of Brown, throughout the narrative. He has sacrificed his ethics and the lives of others to overcome Brown and win over Susan. Now Diamond has exposed the full evil of Brown's life to Susan and seen his nemesis captured. For Alton the technical challenge was simple: "Fog photographs lighter than it looks to the eye. Actors are dressed in dark wardrobe, so that they stand out against the back haze . . . with a remarkable third-dimensional feeling. Fog is particularly suitable for outstanding light effects in the form of shafts of light." When they reproduced this image, Place and Peterson extrapolated further that "silhouetted figures standing in a rigid position become abstracted Modern Man and Woman. . . . The backlighting of heavy smoke and an ominously circling light visible in the background further abstracts the environment into a modern nether world."

Certainly metaphor and abstraction are parts of this image. But the stylistic implications are much more direct and keyed to the emotional states of the characters. As noted, the viewer knows who these people are and what they feel but not how their relationship will be resolved. In classical usage, fog does not enshroud the nether world itself but the transitional locus, the passageway between worlds. Clearly Lowell and Diamond are poised on the brink of something new. The fog separates them from the physical reality of the world outside the hangar. Highlights kick off the edge of the doorway reinforcing this sense of movement out into open space. As they exit, nothing except a forlorn wheelbarrow in the left foreground is clearly visible. Their movement towards the shaft of light suggests an elemental behavior: emotionally spent they walk in the direction of the brightest spot at the center of the frame. While they move at the same time, they are not together, and the distance between them is exaggerated by what Alton calls the "third-dimensional feeling." The viewer may assume that, since they are both going to the light, they will rejoin there. But, as the figures disappear into the fog, as they begin the transition, nothing is certain.

If there is any assumption which we make about the noir style, it is simply that those filmmakers who created it understood, like Alton, what they were creating and that resulted in a unique body of films. Through those films, film noir demonstrates a style in its purest form, a style that viewers then and now perceived without the need for any superimposed indicators. As we first suggested in *Film Noir: An Encyclopedic Reference to the American Style*, one might consider a random selection of motion pictures released over an eighteen month period such as *The Big Clock* (Paramount, 1948), *Brute Force* (Universal, 1947), *Cry of the City* (20th Century-Fox, 1948), *Force of Evil* (MGM, 1948), *Framed* (Columbia, 1947), *Out of the Past* (RKO, 1947), *The Pitfall* (United Artists, 1948), and *The Unsuspected* (Warner Bros., 1947)—films that employed eight different directors, eight different cinematographers, and eight different screenwriters adapting eight different original stories for different stars at eight different studios. These people of great and small technical reputations created eight otherwise unrelated motion pictures with one cohesive style.

Jean Wallace and Cornel Wilde in The Big Combo (1955).

Fred Astaire and Cyd Charisse in The Bandwagon (1957).

Today what simpler demonstration could there be of a style's existence than a conscious homage or parody? Long before *Dead Men Don't Wear Plaid*, even before the classic period of film noir ended, there were obvious moments such as the 1957 "Girl Hunt Ballet" in *The Bandwagon*. In the 90s, neo-noir films rife with allusions to the classic period have become a favorite genre of filmmakers and the sharpest noir parodies are in comic books and television commercials.

Like the "Girl Hunt Ballet" before it, *Fatal Instinct* (1993) is a satire of the conventions of the classic period. In a neo-noir context, where many of this generations filmmakers have taken elements of the classic period style and created a genre, the parody of *Fatal Instinct* crystallizes many of the icons and motifs which constitute the noir style, and which will be dealt with later in this book, motifs which drew from the cinema's relationship to other styles such as graphics and fashion. The setting is classic noir: a dimly lit club in the heart of the urban jungle at night. A femme fatale (Sean Young) with obligatory cigarette and drink, ubiquitous props in the noir universe, blows smoke in the face of her potential victim (Armand Assante). She wears a low-cut, slinky gown and sports peroxide hair with a fashionable flip, marking her as a noir "spider lady." Setting and lighting complete the mock style.

It is not the purpose of this book to approach film noir from an auteurist or any other polemical perspective. Style is an evanescent thing and, as the discussion of *The Big Combo* confirms, permits variant readings; but any reading implies a writer. Place and Peterson reproduced an image from an early film noir with the following comment: "Bogart finally realizes it is Lupino he loves in *High Sierra* [1941]. The low-placed key light creates a stark lighting in which interior feelings of the characters are finally exposed and laid bare." In this instance their reading goes directly to the dramatic situation of which the viewer is already aware. Bogart's character, "Mad Dog" Roy Earle, has never thought of Lupino's Marie as more than a moll. The "low placed key light" is not near the floor, not what Alton called "criminal lighting . . . a low light which illuminated the face from an unusual angle [so that] it distorted the countenance." In this example, the light is designed to match the source, an oil lamp in the center foreground. Since the figures stand close to it, they block off the rest of the room, the walls and ceiling of which are an out-of-focus dark gray behind them. Thus alone in the foreground of the two dimensional frame, the lamp itself separates them; but Earle reaches across it to touch Marie's face. Being closest to the light, Bogart's palm is quite bright, and the light seems to flow up from it into Lupino's face, underscoring the emotional bond which the gesture first reveals. Moreover, while both faces

Armand Assante and Sean Young in Fatal Instinct (1993).

are brightly lit, the features are still modeled. Bogart's expression reflects his character's sympathy and concern because Marie has been struck in the face by someone else. Lupino makes Marie's expression at once apprehensive and hopeful. The bruise on her face barely mars her features. The light actually smoothes her skin, accents her lips, eyes, and thin brows, and throws a halo of highlights on her carefully coifed hair. What Bogart sees is an extremely attractive young woman, whose physical beauty and emotional empathy he had ignored because of the circumstances under which they met.

The survey of the noir style which follows makes no critical argument and follows no preconceived progression. From thousands of possibilities, the images were selected not because they are from the "best" noir films but rather because they best exemplify an aspect or aspects of the noir style. And, of course, we have mostly used production stills which more sharply render the graphic impact of film noir in a single image and not frame enlargements which most accurately render actual frames from any film. Overall, we have grouped the chapters to reflect certain motifs prevalent in the cycle and tried to allow the images to speak for themselves first. We would hope that one could just leaf through this book, ignoring our comments entirely, and still come away with a clear sense what the noir style is all about. Place and Peterson asked "without the film before us...how can we discuss style?" As commentators, we must allow for some extrapolation, we must as needed fill in the dramatic context of a motion picture for a reader who has only a single image as a referent. Within that single image lies only part of the story and part of the style. Ultimately, our hope is that viewers/readers of this book find inspiration to become viewers, again or for the first time, of the classic noir films themselves.

Humphrey Bogart and Ida Lupino in High Sierra (1941).

CHAPTER ONE

OUT OF THE PAST

The socio-cultural precedents for film noir are many and diverse. Most commentators have compiled lists of the aesthetic and social underpinnings of film noir. The usual suspects were and are German Expressionism and the European émigrés who came to Hollywood to escape Nazism; hard-boiled fiction and the alienated post-World War II populations; realist painters and improved film stocks and production equipment. While the cause-and-effect relationships for the emergence of film noir as a whole and the refinement of its visual style in particular are not absolute, there are many clear influences inside and outside of the motion picture industry.

FOR ANTHONY JOHN (RONALD COLEMAN) IN *A DOUBLE LIFE* (1948) the problem lies in the pasts of others, the pasts of characters whose lives he impersonates on stage and cannot leave behind him there. This shot of John in the portrait gallery of the theater lobby encapsulates his emotional position. Caught in the light from a just opened door, John is frozen between two portraits. Behind him his elongated shadow touches the edge of a portrait in modern dress, wearing a trench coat with a turned-up collar not unlike the one that covers him in the present, caught by the light and brightly illuminated at frame center. Directly before him is a radically different image: the twisted Richard III, captured with a dagger in one hand and the grasping fingers of the other distended in avarice or anguish, posed like a distorted reflection of the real John, whose hand is held up clutching a cigarette. This portrait of John as Richard is physically unlike the man caught in the light, but emotionally it is a much truer reflection. While it is Othello who ultimately captures John's soul and leads to his real suicide while in character on stage, John as Richard projects the turmoil inside the actual man.

WHILE THE PHRASE "GERMAN EXPRESSIONISM" MAY BE USED TO CHARACTERIZE diverse plastic and literary works, its association with film typically evokes a prototype like *The Cabinet of Dr. Caligari*, where an angular and chiaroscuro visual style supports an oneiric, surrealistic narrative. Hollywood filmmakers had always used such elements in diverse genres.

The 1930 adaptation of *Dr. Jekyll and Mr. Hyde* has stylistic uses similar to many noir films. In the shot of Hyde (Fredric March) in the doorway, the staging creates a sense of constriction as the figure is hemmed in by the door and frame. The lighting adds more layers. The low side light flares off the figure's face, shirt front, and in the foreground, his hand on the knob. The already twisted features are more grotesque under the harsh light which brings out the simian brow and gaping mouth. The banister shadow which cuts the frame horizontally is also constricting. But if it symbolizes the social constraints on most people's behavior, this atavistic figure easily breaks it as a slight angle captures him leaning forward menacingly.

N COMPARISON, THE 1932 *OLD DARK HOUSE* RELIES MORE HEAVILY on stagecraft. The bars through which the butler Morgan (Boris Karloff) menaces Gladys DuCain (Lillian Bond) were certainly an important motif in film noir, but the physical elements in this shot undergo scant modulation from the lighting or angle. The actress's expression clearly registers fear, but Morgan's hand thrust through the bars would seem to be out of her field of vision. The bright fill light on her figure and the stone wall, the open space on three sides of her, and the eye-level camera angle all further diminish the sense of peril, while the dark bars which cut through the butler's figure and obscure his face seem firmly to restrain him.

ALSO IN 1930, PAUL MUNI STARRED AS TONY CAMONTE IN *SCARFACE*. IN THIS SHOT OF Camonte in a drawing room the ostensible source light casts shadows of window frames and curtains on the back wall and highlights the right side of Camonte's suit. Camonte is a Capone-like mob boss, whose sociopathic resolve is as clear from his narrow-eyed gaze and the shadow of a hand which becomes a fist on his coat front as from the steel-plated door behind him, which is meant to keep bullets from riddling his sanctuary. Camonte's henchman Angelo (Vince Barnett) leans against the door as if pushed back by the sheer force of Camonte's will.

While not part of a rigid continuum, the gangster and horror film in 1930 were both part of the pre-noir style in Hollywood. March's Mr. Hyde was less mannered than John Barrymore's ten years earlier and less intellectual than Spencer Tracy's ten years later. As a creature from id, all three Hydes can be seen as linked to the disturbed protagonists of noir; but the 1930 film is the one which bridges the Expressionistic and noir styles. Similarly, gangster films of the silent era such as *The Racket* (1927) or Von Sternberg's *Underworld* (1927) and *Thunderbolt* (1929) created a stylistic base for all the early sound gangster films, *Little Caesar* and *Public Enemy* as well as *Scarface*.

ADECADE LATER, HYDE WAS STILL HYDE BUT THE GANGSTER PROTAGONIST HAD ONE FOOT in the nascent noir tradition. In The Roaring Twenties (1939) George Hally (Humphrey Bogart) and Eddie Bartlett (James Cagney) are both veterans of the same World War I outfit and both ultimately become rival bootleggers. The Wall Street crash and the end of prohibition wipe out Bartlett, who confronts Hally to protect a former girlfriend and a third war buddy. As a character who suffers mischances and dies trying to redeem himself, Bartlett resembles many noir protagonists. But the visual style of The Roaring Twenties is still merely pre-noir. While a high-key rim light does kick off the figure's head as Bartlett confronts Hally with a drawn revolver, the relatively bright fill light illuminates the rear wall, including the side-bar and the prints with an oddly-Western motif.

WHILE THE HORROR FILM IN THE 1940S WAS MOSTLY GIVEN OVER TO PARODIES starring Bob Hope or Abbott and Costello, the "serious" productions did not progress stylistically from their 1930s antecedents. Although directed by Robert Siodmak, Son of Dracula (1943) relies more on special effects and set dressing than lighting or framing. In the final scene, Frank Stanley (Robert Paige) prepares to immolate the body of his undead fiancée Katherine Caldwell (Louise Albritton). While the trappings of the room from the coffin to the bed canopy are elaborate and detailed, the light filtered through the curtains is muted and full. Six months before directing the landmark noir films Phantom Lady and Christmas Holiday back to back, Siodmak relied mostly on fog machines and white make-up to add visual flair to Son of Dracula.

HERVE DUMONT GAVE HIS CRITICAL BIOGRAPHY OF ROBERT SIODMAK THE SUB-TITLE "Master of Film Noir"; but Siodmak's interaction with the noir style, like that of Fritz Lang or Anthony Mann or any of the filmmakers of the classic period, is part of a collective event. One of the strongest candidates for the seminal film in terms of the noir style is *Citizen Kane (1941)*. The manipulation of all the elements—angle, framing, lighting, mise-en-scène, camera movement, duration of shot, optical effects, and montage—made *Citizen Kane* a compendium of visual style. Certainly there is little if anything in *Citizen Kane*, from its depth of field to its optical masking of miniatures, which is entirely original, but it is the application of style with a consistent, and insistent, intentionality that, more than any other single motion picture, anticipates the entire noir movement. As Charles Foster Kane (Orson Welles) rails after Boss J.W. "Big Jim" Gettys (Ray Collins), a variety of elements in the shot interact with the depth of field. The latter does hold the two figures together, even as Gettys descends the stairs, inside the unusually deep plane of focus. Although the petulant Kane leans forward of the guard rail, his figure is smaller and askew, his arm out at an unnatural angle. Compared to the upright figure as he moves down the stairs, Kane is weak and imbalanced. A key light strikes Kane from above, highlighting the graying and receding hairline as its seems to push down on his form and bend it at the waist. The oblique line of the wall at left also seems to push against Kane. A different key light strikes Gettys from below casting a shadow from his shoulder across his face which seems to brace his resolve. He slides along the strong diagonal of the banister, the line of which veers up in the back almost touching Kane's hand. The rail serves as a metaphor for the fixed course from which Kane cannot deter Gettys. While only waist high, the guardrail and banister posts in front of Kane hold him back, entrap him as he is powerless to stop Gettys.

CONCURRENT MOVEMENTS IN LITERATURE, THEATER AND ART PUT AN emphasis on realism. Some of the most literal images of the nocturnal, urban landscape were recorded by Arthur H. (Usher) Fellig, better known as Weegee, who roamed the streets of New York City at night looking for sensationalist photo-ops. His work and that of Morris Engel added grimness and shock value to the proletarian work of Paul Haviland ("Luna Park, 1909") and Walker Evans ("Negro Barber Shop"). The "blood on the pavement" school was a stark contrast to the traditional aesthetic in work of Ansel Adams or Cecil Beaton. It was the Weegee style of street scene which Elmer Rice and Clifford Odets dramatized; which Hemingway, Hammett, and Chandler evoked in prose; which Edward Hopper and Reginald Marsh painted in somber hues.

Marsh's proletarian canvasses reflected the travails of the post-Depression lower class. His Bowery series probed the lower depths of urban America. In *Smoke Hands* (1934), a bowery street under the El tracks is bustling with activity well into the night. While two men try to get a drunken central figure to his feet and two others look on, many more—a crowd both nearby and farther in the background—seem to take no notice. Two men on the right seem to be sharing their own bottle; another on the left stares sullenly across the street. Is he disinterested or disgruntled because his drunken associate took the last swig before collapsing? A lit display for a tattoo parlor is overhung by the stark white cross of the All Night Mission, the sign for which is nearly dead center in the image.

The pose of Stella (Linda Darnell), the ambitious small-town waitress, in *Fallen Angel* (1946) captures the same determination to survive as the Marsh figures. Her outfit from frilly hat to ribboned shoes is the best she can do. The shoes may pinch her feet, but they cannot crush her hopes. The background in the diner, the cheap tablecloth and the sign announcing the special price for chicken-fried steak quickly define the milieu. Stella's clothes confirm that she is poor but determined to make an impression. The softened key light shimmers off her legs and smoothes her face, which is the center of interest in the frame. Her glance upward confirms that life has not been easy but that she has not given up hope.

Courtesy of the Corcoran Gallery of Art

Edward Hopper's *Drug Store* (1927) uses merely a dark cityscape and signage to create many of the same emotions as Marsh's images of the Bowery. The vertical sign that probably reads "drugs" is cut off, so that only part of the "G" and the "S" can be seen; the name and street number for "Silber's Pharmacy" are plainly visible but dark. At visual center, the display window, so brightly lit that it illuminates the sidewalk in the foreground, introduces more ironic counterpoints: the unpleasant connotations of illness and constipation proclaimed by the words "PRESCRIPTIONS DRUGS" and "EX-LAX" are over what seems to be a display of gift boxes. The light surfaces inside the store window are surrounded by dark streets and building facades. The frame (right) from *Thieves' Highway* (1949) illustrates the further transformation of elements from Marsh

and Hopper into classic period film noir. At left, Mike Figlia (Lee J. Cobb) stands in front of a produce stand that displays his name as proudly as "Silber's" and speaks with a tall woman, Midgren (Hope Emerson). Meanwhile seller Nick Garcos (Richard Conte, right) stands nearby while other figures inside are absorbed in their own tasks. As in the Hopper, the source light from under the sign (in this case, work lights inside the stand) illuminates everything else and throws sharp highlights onto the faces of the characters. As in Marsh the characters' gazes and postures belie a possible connection between them all. In fact, the injured Garcos is about to confront Figlia for misappropriating his goods. The vendor, in turn, is hemmed in by the boxes of produce, the buying and selling of which control his behavior and drive his greedy exploitation of the truck farmers who come to him.

LTHOUGH EDWARD HOPPER PAINTED SUCH PRE-NOIR CANVASES AS *DRUG STORE*, *AUTOMAT*, and *Night Windows* in the 1920s, the better-known *Nighthawks* (1942) is an image that could easily be mistaken for a film noir lobby card. According to Hopper biographer Gail Levin, the figures in *Nighthawks*—a starkly realistic painting of three patrons (a couple and a solitary man with his back to the viewer) and a uniformed counterman in a late night diner—was inspired by Hemingway's "The Killers." In Robert Siodmak's 1946 film adaptation of the Hemingway short story, the title characters arrive at a local diner in the first scene. From their expressions Al (Charles McGraw) and Max (William Conrad) are not ordinary travelers. In the title sequence just preceding, they have walked determinedly down the dark streets of the small town towards the island of light represented by the diner, much as in Hopper's painting. As they talk to the bartender about the whereabouts of a local man named Swede, the decorative lights cast ominous shadows on the ceilings above. The same source light throws dark shadows from the hat brims down to their browlines, isolating their smooth, unsmiling faces and manicured hands on the counter. The array of commonplace items, the napkin and condiment dispensers, the water pitcher and the white-suited counterman, play against the darkness outside and its undertone of menace.

HE SYMBIOTIC RELATIONSHIP BETWEEN THE OTHER VISUAL ARTS AND FILM noir is apparent in graphic arts as well: posters for noir films, comic strips such as Will Eisner's "The Spirit," animated films like Max Fleischer's *Superman* series, and pulp magazine and novel cover illustrations. This book cover for the pulp detective fiction *Louis Beretti* dates from the late 1940s. All of the icons which typify noir are present. It is night in the city on a bridge with the skyline of Manhattan in the background. A femme fatale, in a clinging and provocative red dress with the de rigueur peroxide hair, stands in the background beneath a lamppost, a pose which often marks the woman as a street walker. She dominates the frame because she stands on the stairs, making her seem taller than the man in the foreground. The look on the face of the man also enhances her power. He glances towards her with fear and suspicion. He is lighting a cigarette, another icon of noir and of the period. Both the flame from the match and the cigarette visually lead the spectator back to the woman's curvaceous body. Even the use of the winding stairs reflects the noir predilection for that particular piece of decor.

THE VISUAL TENSION OF EVERYDAY ITEMS AND EXTRAORDINARY events is a frequent ironic motif in film noir. The supermarket scene from *Double Indemnity* (1944) is a perfect example. Walter Neff (Fred MacMurray) and Phyllis Dietrichson (Barbara Stanwyck) have conspired to kill her husband and cannot chance having a private rendezvous observed, so they arrange to be in the same aisle of a local market. The meticulously ordered array of packaged goods as well as the sign for "quality foods" are unrelentingly mundane and easily read as symbols of the ordinary and ordered world in which most people live. For Phyllis, the sunglasses shield her eyes and her possible hidden motives from Neff. His expression is telling, glancing over despairingly at her as she looks straight ahead. Trapped, almost completely enveloped in the two dimensions of the frame, these killers are discomfited not by their guilt but by their fear of discovery, dependent on each other's nerve but uncertain if they can count on it.

REFINEMENT OF A THEME

As film noir's classic period entered what Paul Schrader called its "second phase" in the years immediately after World War II, the sense of a dark, inescapable past became a prime theme. By 1947 films such as *Body and Soul*, *The Locket*, *Nightmare Alley*, *Ride the Pink Horse*, and *Dead Reckoning* all elaborated on this theme, but none so powerfully as the most aptly titled *Out of the Past*.

FILM NOIR'S MOST IRONIC IMAGES NEED NOT BE ITS DARKEST. IN THIS shot from *Out of the Past* (1947), Jeff Bailey (Robert Mitchum) and his fiancée Ann (Virginia Huston) seem to be caught in a tender moment by an idyllic lakeside setting. But the past has reached out and found Bailey hiding in Bridgeport, California and its emotional presence permeates the sequence. As Bailey ponders what he must do, his expression is clearly preoccupied and concerned. He sits awkwardly on a fallen log, his body twisted with one leg up and shoulders hunched down, reaching out to Ann, who represents his hope for a new life. He rests one hand on hers and another on her back but is unable to embrace her. The body, in fact, hems Bailey, pushes him back in the two dimensions of the frame against another weathered tree trunk. Her look is not as troubled but pensive. Neither of them face towards the clear open waters of the lake and its promising expanse. Instead they stare at something out of frame, that unknown something out of the past which has suddenly threatened their future.

EQUALLY DISTURBING WITHOUT BEING OBVIOUSLY SO IS THE IMAGE FROM *CHRISTMAS Holiday* (1944). Abby Manette (Deanna Durbin) confronts her ne'er-do-well husband Robert (Gene Kelly, right). Although his arm is at his side and his figure not too close to hers, something in Robert's expression or bulk seems to press her back against the wall. While neither figure seems aware of the others who are at the left edge of the shot, those characters all regard Abby and Robert quite pointedly if not warily. The emotional vortex is most clearly revealed in Abby's face at frame center. With one hand holding to the edge of the wall and the other behind her, Abby's head is pressed back against the wall paper, clinging to it as forcefully as the painted vines. She looks unflinchingly at Robert while the key light, hitting her from hairline to shoulders, gives her expression a hint of fatigue. By her left arm, the sharp shadow of Robert's hat brim hovers like a dark blade. Other objects, possibly a window frame or tree branches, cut the light into wedges and form a dark bar pressing down on Abby from above. While she could easily turn and retreat from Robert, even insulate herself behind the others, something holds her at the edge of the wall, something likeliest to be the same dark past.

THE DOLEFUL FATE OF STANTON CARLISLE (TYRONE POWER) IN *Nightmare Alley* is effectively self-inflicted. Carlisle's greed compels him to take more risks and manipulate his collaborators in his fake spiritualist act, until he is exposed and reduced to working as a carnival "geek." Although he photographed less than a dozen film noir, Lee Garmes helped apply a classic chiaroscuro to the troubled surroundings of protagonists in many types of melodrama. The simple "north light" as Carlisle ponders his fate in *Nightmare Alley* needs no further manipulation. Powers's look of resignation is molded by the light, which reveals the clenched muscle in his jaw. The hand clutching a cigarette is held thoughtlessly, below his field of view. In the background, a tangle of poles, wires, and hanging lights loom darkly over Carlisle. The same unseen source light catches the other carnival denizen Pete (Ian Keith), as he steps from behind the canvas. His furrowed brow, tangled hair, and half his face in darkness as he regards Carlisle give him the aspect of an evil angel. Most telling is the pint bottle in the man's left hand, a way to obliterate the past with its promise glistening in the transparent shadow at the center of the frame.

GARMES ALSO PHOTOGRAPHED *CAUGHT* (1949) FOR DIRECTOR MAX Ophuls. Leonora Eames (Barbara Bel Geddes) has fled her unhappy marriage to a wealthy paranoiac and found happiness working for Dr. Larry Quinada (James Mason). Conflicted because she carries her husband's child, Leonora allows herself to be sucked back into an abusive relationship with him. For Ophuls the sense of fateful linkages is often expressed by a fluid camera and long takes; but static images can also emphatically define emotional conditions. Leonora's obvious vacillation is captured in her knitted brow and her pose with her hand nervously brought up to her mouth. Quinada's posture reflects his desire to console and reassure her, his look of patient concern maintained even though she is glancing elsewhere. They stand framed in low angle against a black emptiness which isolates them and offers nowhere to flee.

Most menacing of all are the two foreground objects: a hand which reaches out towards Leonora, its shadow already clutching at her shoulder, fingers distended as if intended for her throat; and, against Quinada's dark coat, an even more ominous firebrand intruding into the shot. Disconnected from the people to whom they are attached, the hand and the brand are reduced to overt symbols, which in the style of film noir embody the pain and disturbance lurking in the unburied past.

MOTIF

Bars

As much of film noir centers on the sense of a fateful, alienating, but unseen force which traps and threatens to literally imprison its protagonists, the visual motifs of entrapment and alienation are central also. A key example is the recurring image of prison-like bars and cage wire—both literal and metaphorical—in so many noir films.

In *Crossfire* (1947), the bars are a secondary motif. In the interrogation of the seated serviceman Montgomery (Robert Ryan, left), the police detective Finlay (Robert Young, right) and Sergeant Keeley (Robert Mitchum, center) flank and dominate him. The harsh light from the hanging lamp over Montgomery casts dark shadows which obscure his eyes, while motivating the use of a complimentary rim light on the other two. Keeley's chiseled features, neatly-knotted tie, and polished belt buckle suggest proper military posture in contrast to the collar-less Montgomery, whose shirt hangs over his belt. Finlay's own tie and tweed suit combine with his pipe and gesture to reinforce his position of authority. The black grid of bars that stops short of the ceiling separates them from a dark wall cut by diagonal light, not from a corridor or other exit. While Montgomery's figure is entirely contained with the rectangle of the bars, Keeley's head rises above them and most of Finlay's figure is beyond their outer edge. As such, the bars, which could be a naturalistic element of decor in a normal police station or interrogation room, become expressionistic, suggesting the trapped and constricted mentality of the bigoted killer Montgomery.

SEVERAL OF THE CRIMINAL CHARACTERS IN *THE BIG COMBO* (1955) STRUGGLE FOR dominance within the frame and within the narrative. In this context, as they wait by a barred passage, all of them are imprisoned by their environment and behavior. The sniveling Mingo (Earl Holliman, right) is the most ill at ease. As he looks around apprehensively, one eye is blocked from view by a bar, another is obscured by the bar's shadow. The confident Fante (Lee Van Cleef, left) casually crosses his arms and raises a hand holding a cigarette; but the irregular shadows on his face distort the lines of his face. Like Mingo, Fante knows that McClure (Brian Donlevy, center) the syndicate boss behind them, will soon be killed but is untroubled by that prospect. Suspecting that Mr. Brown, Mingo and Fante's chief, has marked him, McClure focuses his gaze on the slicker Fante. The unbroken light on the older man's face suggests that some residue of his power remains.

ALTON ASSERTS IN *PAINTING WITH LIGHT* THAT "EVEN IN DAYLIGHT SCENES... LIFE IN captivity is dark...a cell window [is] high up on the wall. Through this window comes a shaft of sunlight to remind one of the precious freedom that exists outside." The fact of the bars' presence establishes a primary and literal reading of a given shot and situation. Under the influence of the noir style this is supplemented by a secondary and figurative embellishment that relies on how that physical presence is staged and lit. Both elements are emphatically present in the shot of Vic (Mark Stevens) from *Cry Vengeance* (1954) late in the classic period. The content is simple: a solitary figure on a jail house cot; the particulars of mise-en-scène and lighting create a host of other implications. The bars are present only in shadow. A high front light renders them sharply along with his figure on the bottom back wall; and they stretch and distort in a grid behind him. Immediately above, the bulky outline of an upper bunk hangs like a dark cloud. At frame center is a vortex of pent-up anger. While a broken bar shadow cuts down his cheek, the brightest spot in the frame is still Vic's face, and the grim determination etched into it is unmistakable. The pictures of the loved ones over whose death he is crying for vengeance are also brightly lit. The character's motivation is subtly refined by two other items. The chain over his shoulder and the cot with its legs touched with highlights in the foreground both convey a sense of rigidity that parallel and augment the pose of Vic's body, suggesting that he will not be dissuaded or deterred from exacting retribution.

At first glance only the literal values are evident in another isolated and imprisoned figure, that of Marie Allen (Eleanor Parker) in the bluntly titled *Caged* (1949). She is caged and her look off-screen is at once imploring and desperate. But the lighting models the gray tones into a range of expressive touches. The thin shadows of the mesh distort so that they seem to tear at her arms and throat like sharp ligatures. The brightest points are her fingertips which claw at the enclosure, a palpable visual metaphor for her trapped, bird-like situation, and are the only vestiges of her body which are outside the cage and "free." The visible source of light is from two windows behind her. Yet highlights strike the panel below her right elbow; and another cuts in brightly above her left hand. They intrude from somewhere outside the frame like rays of hope and bounce onto her figure and rim light her shoulders and the top of her head.

Lovers separated when one of them is imprisoned is a common plot in film noir. The framing and decor when they meet in prison often anticipates their fate. In Fritz Lang's bleak late noir, *Beyond a Reasonable Doubt* (1956), Susan Spencer (Joan Fontaine) visits her fiancè Tom Garrett (Dana Andrews). Although Susan and the viewer believe that Tom is innocent of the murder for which he has been condemned—that, in fact, he incriminated himself as part of a journalistic stunt in concert with Susan's father—the elaborate wall which separates them is emblematic of what has and what will happen. Tom had planned to use Susan's father to exonerate him after he actually does kill his ex-wife. His "tangled web" is as complicated as the decor, bars, two types of grillwork, and solid, bolted metal, which separate the figures. In Lang's deterministic vision, that web which imprisons Tom now foreshadows Susan's discovery of his guilt and her decision not to produce the exculpatory documents which her father had prepared before his death.

This effect is even more subtly realized in Lang's earlier, pre-noir *You Only Live Once* (1937), when Jo Graham (Sylvia Sidney) goes to meet her fiancé Eddie Taylor (Henry Fonda) before his release. Although both are happy at the prospect of his impending release, the grim reality of Eddie's past dooms both of them. The bars which hold him physically will never let him escape from the fatal trap in which so many of Lang's characters are caught, and the couple's momentary happiness will end in their death as fugitives. In this context, Jo's smiling face which is thrust through the bars to almost touch Eddie's equally ecstatic visage renders the core irony of film noir's fugitive couples.

In contrast, the jail house meetings between Carol "Kansas" Richman (Ella Raines) and her condemned boss Scott Henderson (Alan Curtis) in Robert Siodmak's adaptation of Cornell Woolrich's *Phantom Lady* (1944) permit unimpeded physical proximity as they smoke cigarettes together. Even as Henderson hangs his head and tells her to forget about him, to abandon him even though he is innocent of the crime for which he is to be executed, her posture and expression confirm that she will not give up. It is her determination which will free him, just as her presence in the shot separates him from the dark bars in the left background and "pushes" him towards the sunlit window, where the bars to freedom are barely visible.

ONE OF THE FINAL SHOTS OF FILM NOIR'S MOST CELEBRATED FUGITIVE COUPLE DOES
not even contain bars. Nonetheless, the reed stalks in which Bart and
Annie Laurie Starr (John Dall and Peggy Cummins) make their final stand
after being surrounded by trackers in Gun Crazy (1950) are even more
visually constricting. Using a set on a sound stage rather than the natural
environment permits a more facile manipulation of certain elements (such
as the fog which surrounded them the previous night). The expressive impact
of the scene on the viewer is innately affected by the artificial-for-natural
staging. The studio lighting, which is less harsh than the real sunlight it sim-
ulated, renders softer key and background lights that resemble the subdued
interior light one might find in a prison. The enmeshment of the two figures
by the reeds and the narrow paths which they have beaten down in walking
to their present positions have the usual connotations of fatality, entrapped
and isolated from each other in the two dimensions of the frame.
While Bart's figure blends in as he crouches down, Annie Laurie's darker suit
visually reinforces her defiant posture as she stands, gun in hand, to face
her pursuers.

MORE TYPICAL EXAMPLES OF THE BAR MOTIF CREATED WITHOUT ACTUAL BARS ARE
in the shots from Hitchcock's Strangers on a Train (1951) and Stanley
Kubrick's The Killing (1956). The bars which separate Bruno Anthony
(Robert Walker, left) and Guy Haines (Farley Granger) are from a decorative gate. It separates the two men as Anthony reveals that he has murdered
Haines' estranged wife and produced her shattered eyeglasses (in Haines's
hand) as proof. Even as Haines, who has been menaced by Anthony since
their chance encounter in the film's first scene, must face the fact that this
sociopath may now have completely derailed his life, the mise-en-scène
foreshadows his survival. It is Anthony who is "behind" the bars, his right fist
clenched but held back by a decorative whorl, his face shadowed, even cut
off by one bar. While Haines holds the incriminating item, his light coat and
the open area behind him distinguish his position from the dark, confined
aspect of Anthony's; and, in fact, it is Anthony who will ultimately fail to
compel Haines to reciprocate for the murder of his wife and perish at the
film's end.

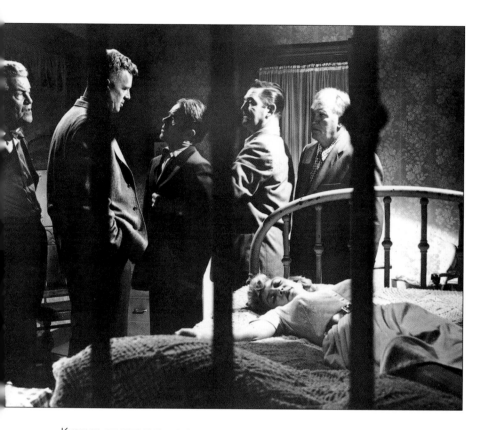

KUBRICK CONSTRAINS HIS CHARACTERS IN THE TWO DIMENSIONS OF THE FRAME WITH an iron headboard which places a set of dark bars across the entire foreground. The conspirators to a racetrack robbery confront the emotionally unstable ticket-clerk Peatty (Elisha Cook, Jr.) next to the body of his wife Sherry (Marie Windsor). As the leader Clay (Sterling Hayden) stares down at the diminutive Peatty, the others array themselves in a way which subtly evokes a line-up, adding another association which foredooms the criminals. The source light from a tipped-over lamp cuts across them diagonally creating hot spots in the mostly dark frame, backlighting the three characters on the right but illuminating the faces of Clay and Unger (Jay C. Flippen). Despite the odd key light, the fixtures of the room are also visible. The crocheted bedspread, the checkered cloth on the end table, the sheers on the windows and the flowery wallpaper all create a sense of the everyday and ordinary, which the foreground object suggests are part of the decor of a large cell.

ANOTHER MIXED METAPHOR IS PRESENT IN THE SHOT FROM ROBERT SIODMAK'S period noir Time Out of Mind (1947): as Kate Fernald (Phyllis Calvert) leans over the balcony and extends her hand towards someone below, no less than three sets of bars cut horizontally through the frame. Before her is the banister, the white spokes of which least resemble prison bars because of their color, shape, and lack of height, not even reaching to the figure's waist. But these spokes and the handrail on which she leans and which prevents her from falling forward also cast two dark shadows. One, low in the frame, falls over a wall and makes the same figurative statement, albeit much less emphatically, as the bars over the wallpaper in The Killing. The more powerful metaphor is above and behind her, a kind of synecdoche in which the shadow suggests the inner state of the character. On the ceiling, the figure and the bar shadows distort and merge, so that the rail cuts across her waist and seems to bend her body, holding her back even as her gesture is elongated and seems more desperate. The low light striking her real figure makes her arm and face the brightest points in the frame and illuminates the white pattern on her blouse. Her gaze is clearly directed below. But on the ceiling above her form is reduced to one dark shade of gray—her gaze, even the direction of the gesture are uncertain. Only the fact that she is somehow restrained by the bars is clear.

NAKED NOIR: WEEGEE AND FILM NOIR

WHETHER OR NOT THERE IS AN INTENTIONAL RELATIONSHIP BETWEEN THE plastic styles of a given era, there are undoubtedly subliminal forces at work which often produce a common aesthetic. Weegee, iconic photographer of life and crime in New York City, published his definitive first book of black-and-white images, *Naked City*, in 1945, at the time that film noir production was nearing its peak in Hollywood. Weegee's photographs are accompanied by his own running commentary, very much like the sardonic, voice-over narration of so many noir films. His photo captions could have the pointedly acerbic pith of Raymond Chandler or the off-handed bite of James M. Cain. In the chapter entitled "Murder," for instance, Weegee wryly observes: "Balcony Seats at a Murder. This happened in Little Italy. Detectives tried to question people in the neighborhood...but they were all deaf...dumb...and blind...not having seen or heard anything."

The audience which so readily embraced noir symbology is much the same as the readers who scanned the tabloids for Weegee's lurid photos. Just after World War II, long after the age of innocence in America, long after a class system had emerged to put the American dream out of reach for many, Weegee's voyeuristic Speed Graphic celebrated the common man and mocked those who led lives of privilege and wealth. Amidst the postwar ennui, underneath a feeling of alienation and boredom, the anti-traditional images of Weegee and film noir both provided a distracting and alternate view of the world.

While Hollywood still produced light-hearted family fare and *The Saturday Evening Post* continued to feature Norman Rockwell covers, Weegee and film noir brought a different reality to both the tabloid pages and the neighborhood screens. *Double Indemnity* was nominated for Best Picture in 1945, but the winner was *Going My Way* starring Bing Crosby and Barry Fitzgerald as priests. The media was at work on consumers who were supposed to abandon war-time frugality for the postwar period of consumption. Hollywood's middle-class characters lived in new tract homes where kitchens were full of shiny new appliances and a new car's finish was safe from the elements in an adjoining garage. By contrast, neither Weegee nor the noir filmmakers bought into the normal aesthetic. Instead they joined the groundswell of anti-traditional expression. As Mike Davis describes it in *City of Quartz*, the choice was between "Sunshine and Noir," a social process by which the vision of noir writers and filmmakers of Hollywood sprang from a phenomenon in which "middle-classes of Southern California became, in one mode or another, the original protagonists of that great anti-myth usually known as noir." On the opposite coast, Weegee followed the same line. He not only eschewed the "beautiful" photograph, but, in fact, he deconstructed middle and upper class values by portraying the superficiality and ugliness of the privileged class. In his series of photos of opera and theater-goers, one of his captions reads: "The common people waited in the street in the rain...for standing room, while Society arrives by taxi wearing galoshes and pearls."

Unquestionably film noir's indigenous and émigré filmmakers alike were influenced by the German Expressionist tradition of the 1920s in art, theater, and film. But can one say the look of the Brücke woodcut or Murnau's *Der Letzte Mann* formed the noir style more vigorously than the realist tradition of black and white still photography popularized by Adams and Stieglitz, where the natural play of light over faces or landscape could so powerfully convey emotion and mood? Weegee's photographs intrude on the quick and the dead alike, inspiring the viewer to participate in his nocturnal excursions, to prowl the night with him and experience the underworld of dark emotions exactly like that of film noir. When a Speed Graphic was too bulky and obvious, he took a pocket camera and infrared film into the unlit recesses to capture people watching movies, milling around fires and crime scenes, huddled in the smoky rear booths of cheap restaurants, aspects of everyday life that normally passed unnoticed.

Weegee remarks on the look of crime scenes in *Naked City*: "They always want to know what paper I'm from and if the person is dead. They seem to be disappointed if they see a sign of life as the stretcher with the injured is carried before them." As with film noir, darker, furtive emotions dictated the aesthetic of his photographs. He was willing to shoot at point blank range in the city's darkest corners, both spellbound and repulsed by the events taking place in front of his lens. As one caption reads "I cried when I took this picture."

Weegee's 1944 photo "Accident on Grand Central Station Roof," exemplifies his own noir style. On a night when the city streets are dampened by rain and fog, he centers on the desolate exterior of train station, a

"Accident on Grand Central Station Roof" (1944)

noir trope wherein a trip acquires associations of loneliness and the unknown. The clock, one-way sign, and the trash can and debris in the foreground complete the noir ambiance, as uniformed police peer down from the roof and two expressionless men in plain clothes—perhaps detectives, perhaps just passers-by—take shelter well behind a crime scene cordon. On top of Grand Central Station, an automobile, another favorite emblem of the era, parked precariously on the roof states that something is awry, lending the same uncomfortable feeling of impending disaster that occurs as one watches the noir film.

"Accident on Grand Central Station Roof" is actually somewhat atypical of many of the photographs that were taken by Arthur (née Usher) H. Fellig (1899-1968), who is still better known by his pseudonymous epithet, "Weegee the Famous." During the late 1930's and early 1940's, when the bulk of his news photos were published, Fellig made Weegee into a noir character in his own right, as he roamed the night in his car, guided by messages on his police radio and some innate compass that lead him to the scene of a crime or a tragedy. Often arriving before the police, Weegee frenziedly captured the first shots of the victims, of their families, of nameless bystanders, of the moment that might change a life or merely mark one's end.

Weegee's career as newspaper photographer, photojournalist and early paparazzo had already taken several turns before he became involved with noir filmmakers. The 1945 publication of *Naked City* got the attention of Hollywood where he spent the years from 1947 to 1952. The art and fashion world recognized Weegee's style as well. *Vogue* retained his services and the Museum of Modern Art acquired several of his photographs giving his tabloid crime illustrations the endorsement of the artistic establishment. During his time on the West Coast, Weegee also collected material for his third book, *Naked Hollywood*, published in 1953.

Weegee's *Naked City* appeared in the same year that Hollywood produced noir films like *Conflict, Mildred Pierce* and *Scarlet Street*. Two years later *Naked City* inspired the film noir by the same name. Producer/narrator Mark Hellinger hired Weegee as a still photographer on a film then called *Homicide*, as a means of acquiring the Weegee title. When finally released in early 1948 Hellinger's *Homicide* had become *The Naked City* (directed by Jules Dassin). Although it won an Academy Award for cinematographer William Daniels (and editor Paul Weatherwax), the look and feel of *The Naked City* is unmistakably Weegee. An easily isolated example is the scene in which children play in the spray of a fire hydrant directly inspired by Weegee's well-known "Summer on Lower East Side," 1937; but throughout the movie the many vignettes of the daily lives of the then 8 million New Yorkers are pure Weegee. Hellinger's introductory voice-over reads like an extended caption from Weegee's book: "We

are flying over an island, a city, a particular city, and this is a story of a number of people and a story also of the city itself. It was not photographed in a studio. Quite the contrary, the actors, played out their roles on the streets, in the apartment houses, in the skyscrapers of New York itself. And along with them, a great many thousands of New Yorkers played out their roles also. This is the city as it is, hot summer pavements, children at play, the buildings in their naked stone, the people without makeup." Hellinger's commentary continues throughout film with an off-handed and often sardonic tone reminiscent of Weegee's captions and recorded remarks.

Weegee received no credit on Hellinger's film, and his spotty association with film noir never brought the fame and recognition that this shameless self-promoter may have been seeking in another medium. In a photograph of himself in front of a poster for the film, it is clear that Weegee's short and stocky physical type recalled the 30's era gangster movies rather than the sleek noir detective. Weegee played a number of bit parts: seamy, New York background characters roles in *The Naked City* and Robert Wise's *The Set Up* (1949). The 1951 *Journey Into Light* aka *Skid Road* (directed by Stuart Heisler,) depicted bums, truck drivers, waitresses, and cops as if taken straight from Weegee's photos. *The Naked City* was adapted for television, and Weegee was a technical advisor on another series, the 1958-59 series *Man with a Camera*, which was inspired by his exploits as a crime photographer. He also was a technical consultant to Stanley Kubrick on *Dr. Strangelove*. After his death Weegee's life and aesthetic inspired the 1992 neo-noir film, *The Public Eye* (directed by Howard Franklin), which opens with classic Weegee images appearing in the developing tray.

Weegee's involvement in noir film was marginal but his influences were significant. Placed side by side, the images of film noir and of Weegee often speak with one voice. Even as the classic noir era ended, location sequences in Aldrich's *Kiss Me Deadly* and Welles' *Touch of Evil* continued to evoke comparisons to his photos. While Weegee's images may never seem staid, much of their shock value has been lost over the past fifty years. Still, his idiosyncratic street photography continues to influence a later generation of photographers such as Garry Winogrand and Diane Arbus and a later generation of filmmakers as well.

"DOA Tied to His Arm" is among Weegee's grislier snapshots. The dark blood splattered on both the pavement and the anonymous man's white shirt and his still-crossed ankles clearly indicate that he was found face down and "left in the gutter." Still hours from daybreak, the residue of blood is already drying in grotesque streaks across his face, like some hideous, over-stated make-up. But this is no Hollywood death, and certainly not how any film, noir or otherwise, could portray it in the 1940s. Compare it to the

"DOA Tied to His Arm"

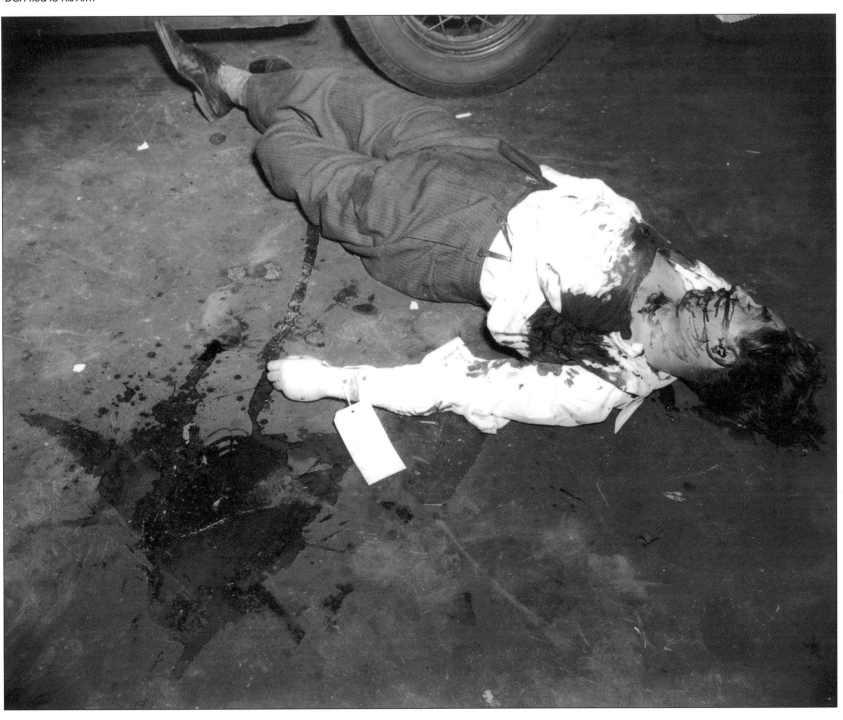

body of Whit Sterling (Kirk Douglas) in *Out of the Past*, lying on a carpeted floor, clothes barely rumpled, and with an off-screen source throwing top-light onto his unmarked face, so that he seems more asleep than dead. In a mise-en-scène where nothing seems out of place, such a placid corpse conjures up nothing more horrible than tranquil repose.

A decade later and some years before he hired Weegee as a technical consultant, Stanley Kubrick returned to his roots as a still photographer and depicted a triple-threat death scene in *The Killing* as Weegee might have done. One body lies face down on a sofa, head buried in the fabric and legs askew and hanging in the air. A second is half on the sofa, half on the floor, right leg bent unnaturally and arm pinched, with blood stains on his forehead and shirt. The third man seems to have been hurled to the carpet along with a table and floor lamp. His coat and pants leg have ridden up with the impact of his fall, and his legs are twisted apart: one lies under the man on the sofa's arm, the other on top of the second victim's shirt. Two streaks trail down each cheek, as if he has wept bloody tears, while the light strikes their lifeless faces from below, accentuating their hellish aspect.

—LINDA BROOKOVER

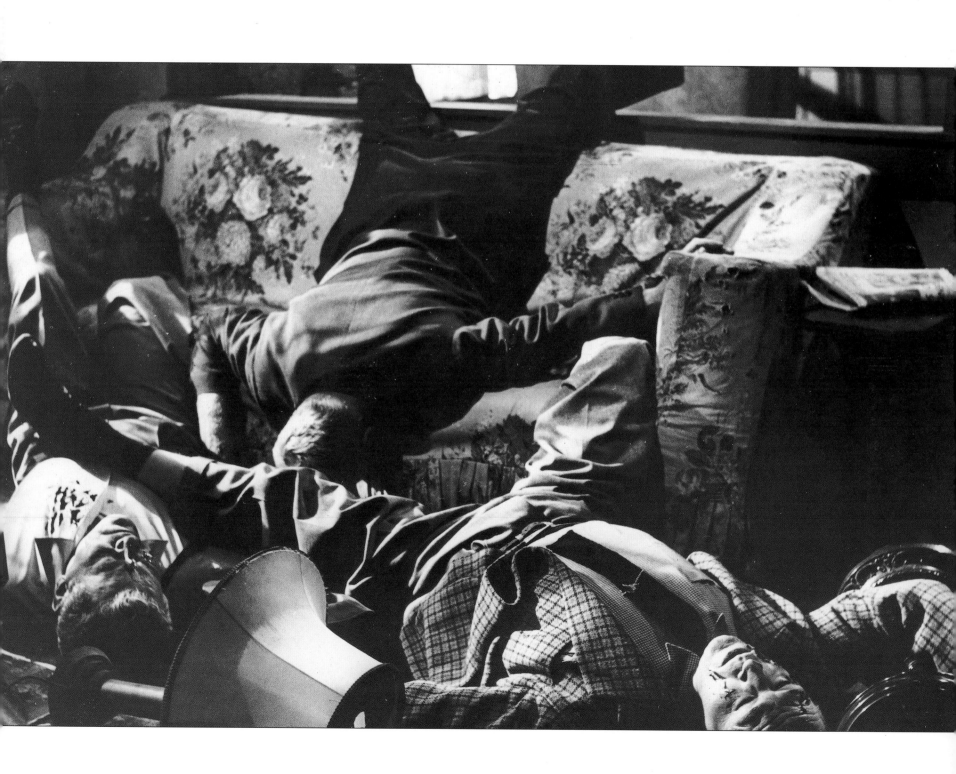

CHAPTER TWO

NIGHT AND THE CITY

A central motif of film noir is the night and the city. Urban landscapes, sometimes crowded, often deserted, sometimes glistening from the rain, always alienating, envelop the characters of noir movies.

THE LONELINESS AND LONGING OF NIGHT IMAGERY PERVADES this shot from *Portrait of Jennie* (1949). Eben Adams (Joseph Cotten) awaits his destiny in the form of a phantom girl, Jennie (Jennifer Jones), seen draped over a bench in the rear of the frame, crying. The painterly lighting of the Central Park scene reflects Adams' own profession as well as the dream world he has entered with this girl who exists in the past and present simultaneously and ages years with each meeting. Adams does not look towards her but out into space as if Jennie is not visible to him yet. An expanse of shadowy pavement separates him from Jennie, symbolizing the barriers of time and space which will ultimately destroy their love. The snow in the far background lit by a single lamppost increases the sense of loneliness with its connotations of isolation. The rounded arch at the top of the frame completes the tableau with an ornamentation redolent of religious paintings.

I N THE APTLY NAMED *NIGHT AND THE CITY* (1950) NE'ER-DO-WELL HARRY FABIAN (RICHARD Widmark), after a hectic encounter with the forces of the city, is comforted by the nurturing Mary Bristol (Gene Tierney). Harry looks disconsolately off to the right of the frame. His body is slumped, his hair tousled, and his suit wrinkled. Mary radiates warmth and caring as she snuggles against his right shoulder, applying, literally and figuratively, a cooling handkerchief to his wounded body and soul. Her expression is one of compassion. As opposed to Harry she radiates optimism with her upturned face, her comforting gesture, and her finely tuned make-up and costume. The tight two-shot also reinforces their intimacy even though Harry looks away off screen.

SHEILA BENNET (EVELYN KEYES) AND MATT CRANE (CHARLES KORVIN) in *The Killer That Stalked New York* (1950) perch precariously on a building ledge. While the city is present only in the faint array of skyscraper lights at the right edge of the frame, the inescapable extrapolation is that its sidewalks also loom far below and that Crane's down-turned eyes focus on them. This corrupt couple who carry the figurative disease of greed as well as the literal one of smallpox are now at the end of their proverbial rope. The mise-en-scène reifies their mutual conflict and distrust. Sheila wears a black tailored suit while Matt sports a light overcoat. Sheila faces toward the walls of the building while her husband faces outwards, pressing his hands against the wall, perhaps recoiling from the brink, perhaps about to push himself him off. While Sheila looks at him with an expression of bitterness, Matt refuses to make eye contact. As he looks to his fate, an unseen light, too bright to be reflected from the city below but unmistakably from that direction, ominously casts his long shadow above him. Even beyond film noir, the conventional associations of low light give any face an eerie, almost demonic aspect, so that he confronts his impending death with the visage of the damned.

I N ANTHONY MANN'S DR. BROADWAY (1942) OPPOSITE EMOTIONS
play out at the same edge of doom. Connie Madigan (Jean
Phillips) has long toyed with disaster in the city for the sake of
tawdry publicity and now stands on the brink of plunging to
her death. The design of the shot is remarkable for its precise
contrast of light and dark elements, the sense of claustrophobic
space in open air, and its ironic relationship to the preceding
narrative. On the left of the frame Connie and her companion
hold on for dear life to the cornice of the building. Its concentric
circular design above their heads intimates at a vertiginous fate
awaiting below. In the two dimensions of the shot, the huge neon
"S" next to them acts as a barrier against the abyss and pins them
visually into that precarious corner. On the right of the frame other
lights, particularly the ad for spearmint gum with blissful fishes
swimming in a neon sea, beckon them ironically. Perhaps the implication of a second chance in the "two trousers" is too subtle to be
intended, but the whole, impersonal array contrasts vividly with the
fear etched in their faces.

THE FUGITIVE COUPLE, TO THE LEFT OF THE FRAME, IN *DUST BE MY Destiny* (1939), Joe Bell (John Garfield) and Mabel (Priscilla Lane), look symbolically and forlornly towards an indefinite future. On the run from prison with the warden's step daughter, Mabel, Joe radiates resolve and forthrightness while Mabel herself seems far less sure of their fate. His arm around his love further reinforces his traditional position as protector. Nick (Henry Armetta), to the right of the frame, shares their concern if not their space. The car isolates him in his own key-lit cubicle, although his concentration is as intense as the couples'. The standard studio city street behind them is deserted, increasing their isolation and vulnerability.

IN *HE RAN ALL THE WAY* (1951) NICK ROBEY (JOHN GARFIELD, RIGHT foreground) ends up in the literal and proverbial gutter of the heartless city. A bar of light along the curb underlines his fate as he grabs his stomach, bleeding his life away. The expression on his face mixes pain with a yearning for some place out of frame, beyond the dirty streets of the city. Directly behind him is his guilt-ridden girlfriend (Shelley Winters) who is responsible for his demise and to her right her father (Wallace Ford), in a trench coat. Both hold guns, the means of Nick's downfall. While the father stands firm in his resolve, the daughter is slumped and ready to collapse, racked by a choice between lover and family. The crowd beyond the three central figures are the faceless denizens of the urban nightmare.

COUPLES IN PERIL CONTINUE WITH ELLEN GRAHAM (VERONICA LAKE) AND PHILLIP RAVEN (Alan Ladd) in This Gun for Hire (1942). The begrimed Ellen seems to merge into the dark bricks to her left and the chiaroscuro train yard behind her. The only highlights on her are her blonde hair, sooty face, and delicately extended left hand holding a monogrammed purse. Raven, the killer who has developed an attachment to Ellen, one of the few people in his life who has befriended him, is a patchwork of light and shadow, externalizing his conflicted nature. He cannot, like Ellen, merge comfortably into the urban landscape. For he is doomed by the forces around him as much as by his psychotic drives. His position slightly to the rear of Ellen makes him visually less imposing. Even though he holds a gun, he seems to be hiding behind her proverbial skirts. She is the protector visually while he is the protected.

SUSAN VARGAS (JANET LEIGH) IN ORSON WELLES' TOUCH OF EVIL (1958) ENCAPSULATES the alienation and isolation of the single noir figure in an urban landscape. She hangs on the edge of the fire escape, crying out for help. Her figure is dwarfed by the facade of a seedy, border town hotel. The double image of the ladder and its own shadow behind her frames her terrified face. Her own shadow is an irregular and cropped mass at the right edge of the frame. While the dull, off-white expanse of wall may symbolize the coldness of the urban environment, the battered fire escape, lit from below to reveal its soiled and rusted underside, makes the precariousness of her situation unmistakable. Even the room behind her to the left of the frame acts as nothing more than a black hole from which this partially clothed "damsel in distress" has escaped only to find herself perched on the brink with a whirlpool of darkness below her.

WET PAVEMENTS, DARKENED STREETS WITH ONLY A LAMPPOST OR SHOW WINDOW TO light the way are quintessential motifs of noir in the city. Cuddles (Dolores Dorn) in Sam Fuller's *Underworld USA* (1960) races through this lonely and potentially menacing environment. Violence is putatively around every corner. It may come from a car to the right of the frame, around a corner to the left of the frame. Even though Cuddles's figure is in the foreground and clearly lit, the surrounding blackness envelopes her. She is vulnerable in her light gray dress, a vulnerability enhanced by her quickened pace and panicked expression. Even her black high-heel pumps add to her image of precariousness with the inherent difficulty of balancing on the slippery pavements.

DETECTIVE JOE BARON (GLENN FORD) IN *THE MONEY TRAP* (1966) grasps at his wounded stomach as he stares at the body of his arch-enemy, Dr. Van Tilden (Joseph Cotten). Baron's trench-coated figure is in an urban landscape recreated on a studio back lot. In this environment the rain can come down and the shafts of light can be arrayed with a precise symmetry that underscores the trench-coated figure's pathetic isolation. Like the women in *Touch of Evil* and *Underworld USA* he is dwarfed by his noir environment. He slumps over, his gun hand drooping at his side. Streaks of light from the lampposts behind him cut the frame horizontally. In the foreground a black car, black fire hydrant, and a black-suited Van Tilden pin him in place as well as block his forward motion visually. This array suggests that he must stagger away towards the light behind him where his own slow death awaits him.

N CONTRAST, THE PERIOD BACK LOT THROUGH WHICH THE LOVELORN composer, George Bone (Laird Cregar) moves is full of asymmetry. While the streetlights of Victorian London in *Hangover Square* (1945) are dimmer and barricades from an excavation stretch diagonally behind him, there is a low source light when he is accosted by a man (Clifford Brooke) who may know he is a killer. The light plays unevenly over the left hand which clutches a ragged bundle and the light coming from below plays unnaturally on both men's faces. As he pulls the lapels of his jacket together to ward off the chill, Bone's own bulk and lighter clothing actually make him seem more vulnerable in the face of the smaller and older man.

BULK ALSO ADDS VULNERABILITY TO DETECTIVE HANK QUINLAN (Orson Welles) in Touch of Evil (1958). Quinlan is a man trapped by the web of violence and deceit he has woven around himself. While his massive figure seems about to explode from an excess of poisonous fluid springing from his corrupt nature, his face sags as he realizes his plans have back-fired and he is now caught in his own web. The frame exhibits several layers of metaphorical traps. In the foreground he is framed by the arch of the porch with its curving designs resembling the jaws of a monstrous animal. Further within the shot the door frame acts as a tighter trap, enclosing his formidable figure. And finally, two shadows cut across his body, one horizontally over his midriff and one diagonally at his knees. These foreshadow his imminent doom. In the background Welles the director places a pair of horns, strategically positioned to give the impression that they are growing out of his head, a none too subtle demonic reference.

N THE CONTEXT OF THE NOIR STYLE, HOW FIGURES ARE POSED CAN POWERFULLY AFFECT MUCH simpler compositions. The poses from both *Where the Sidewalk Ends* (1950) and *The Killers* (1946) are mannered and artificial but graphically evocative. The artifice of the publicity shot of Edmond O'Brien as insurance investigator Frank Riordan in *The Killers* is obvious. The "brick wall" seems clearly thrown up at an odd angle against one with a textured surface, The "red" has been chipped off many of the bricks and several near his face reveal a bulging seam. The source of the low light is equally unnatural. If this is a city street, what light would exist a few feet off the ground? Is this an alleyway with a character caught in a car's head lamps? Where then is the other shadow? Riordan's hand is thrust so vigorously into his jacket pocket that he must be pretending to have a gun. Why? Peterson and Place used a cropped version of this still to illustrate the shadow as "an alter ego, a darker self who cohabits that frame's space." If anything, the edge of the distorted shadow cast on the white wall is so full of jagged angles that it could only be an emotional, not a physical, doppelganger. For all the staged elements, it is O'Brien's look and gesture in the context of night and the city, which give the image a dramatic validity. Whether he is on a sidewalk, in an alleyway, or at the scene dock, the character's glance backward into the flat, low light is unmistakably apprehensive. What he sees, and the viewer does not see, the unknown lurking behind him, outside the frame, creates the tension in the shot. His answering gesture, pretending to be armed, underscores the unseen threat.

THE LIFELESS FORM OF KEN PAINE (CRAIG STEVENS) WHICH DETECTIVE MARK DIXON (Dana Andrews) is preparing to throw in the river in *Where the Sidewalk Ends* is a truer noir alter ego than any shadow. For the murderous cop, the dead criminal represents not just his own crime but what he has become. This other, criminal self is both a literal and figurative burden of which he wants to rid himself. Using a pier on a sound stage permits a precise staging where light from some unseen source glints off spars and oil drums but falls mostly on the two figures in front of a dark process screen. Twice photographed and reduced to two dimensions, the city and river behind Dixon are eerily foreshortened and effectively reinforce his alienation from both natural and artificial landscapes. The bridge looms overhead, not as a promise of passage out of this nightmare but simply as a dark menacing wedge. Even as he looks down at the tangle of ropes, pulleys, and scrap iron that will anchor the body, Dixon knows that he himself is perched fatefully, one misstep away from being cast into the dark waters with his victim. Those dark waters are in their artifice and physical unreality, all the more emotionally real in the noir vision of night and the city.

CITIES CAN ALSO BE PLACES TEEMING WITH ACTIVITY, PLACES WHERE A noir protagonist can lose him/herself in the constant whirl of excitement. In this still from *Phenix City Story* (1955) the spectator encounters a town out of control. The movement of the figures lack any pattern. They move in or face a multitude of directions, creating a visual chaos. In addition, the cracked curb in the foreground, the tawdry facade of the Poppy Club in the background (with its name connoting drugs) as well as the burgeoning fight between the two figures in the middle of the frame—all evoke an urban nightmare common to many noir films. Corruption and violence holds sway in this world as figures of authority, police and the military, stand by unable or unwilling to regulate it.

A MORE ORDERLY VISION OF THE CITY APPEARS IN SAM FULLER'S *THE Crimson Kimono* (1959), a story of crime and a personal relationship between two detectives that is ultimately tinged with racism. A key sequence takes place during a festival, where a line of Japanese-American dancers parades along a downtown street. Their line extends gracefully from the foreground to the background in a powerful diagonal. The elaborate kimonos and the traditional decorations, the paper lanterns and cloth banners, on the streets of Little Tokyo, Los Angeles also create an ambiance of elegance. The women with their make-up and carefully coifed hair walking on their sandaled feet and gesturing in a synchronized dance, represent a link between cultures and the surface order of any society. But under that surface, under the ancient ritual, is the corruption which haunts most noir cities. Part of that pervasive threat lurking in the dark city is revealed when a police chase intrudes on the parade route. Beyond that particular event, that disruption bespeaks the racism, greed, and violence which pervade this film's universe much as it did the worlds of *Touch of Evil* and *Phenix City Story* before it.

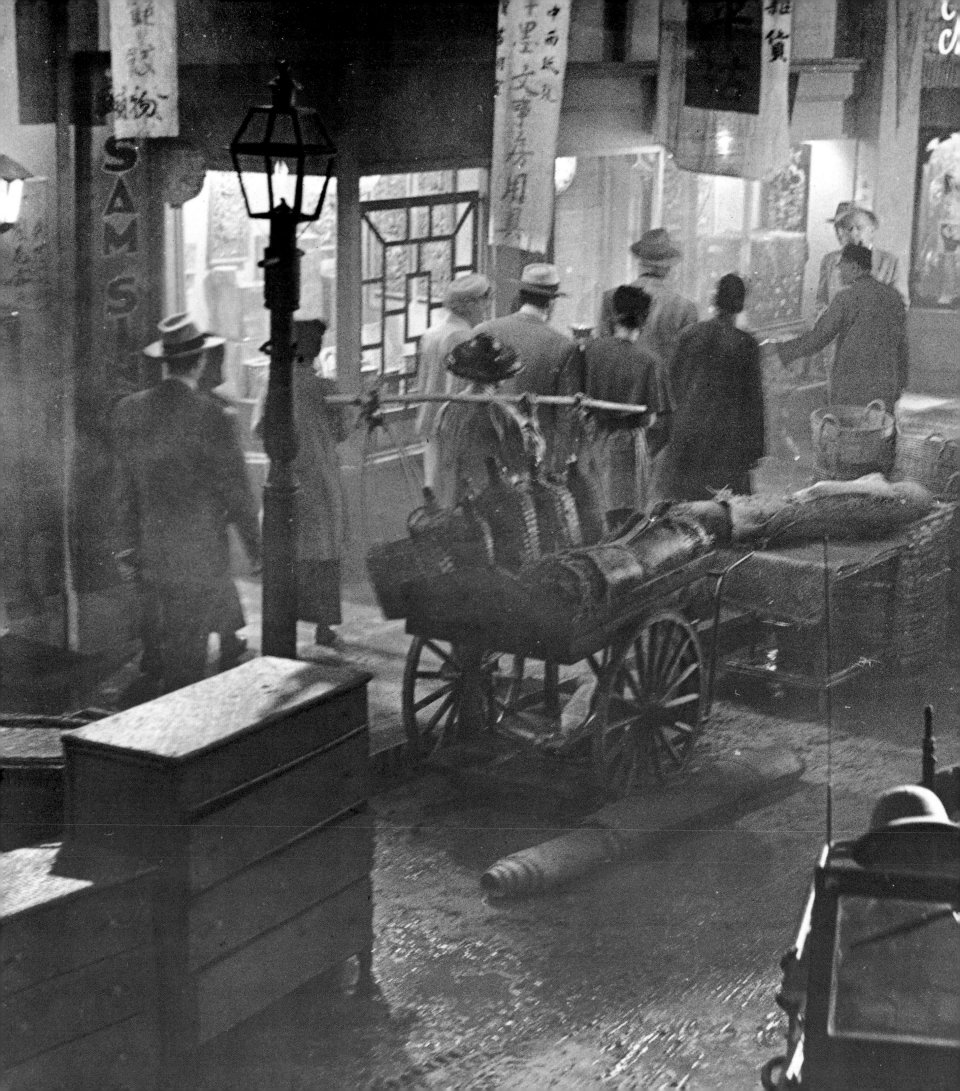

ROM FAUX ASIAN CITIES IN THE WEST (LITTLE TOKYO) TO THEIR antecedents in the East: Singapore in *World for Ransom* (1954) bears the familiar earmarks of a noir den of iniquity. The traffic, both pedestrian and auto, is more orderly than in *Phenix City Story*, with the exception of conflicting lines of movement on the sidewalk, but both have their own "Poppy Club" (here called "The Golden Poppy"). The congestion in the shot indicates the chaos beneath the facade of order. A military jeep in the foreground with the barrel of a rifle clearly visible portends danger and violence. A pall of smoke hangs over the street, adding to a sense of claustrophobia already present in the press of pedestrians, cars, carts, and storefronts. In fact, there is very little space in this frame as almost all areas of the street appear occupied, leaving little breathing room for an already anxious noir protagonist.

MOTIF

Night at the Wheel

FOR THE NOIR PROTAGONIST, NIGHT IN THE CITY OFTEN MEANS A TRIP BY CAR. While the encapsulated interior of the vehicle may give those within a sense of security, that sense often proved, even before car-jacking became a commonplace term, a misguided one. For Gil Bowen (Frank Lovejoy) and Ray Collins (Edmond O'Brien), en route to Mexico for a fishing vacation, the noir nightmare begins when they give a ride to the psychopathic title character in The Hitchhiker (1953). Before their encounter, the inside of their sedan does seem a comfortable haven. RKO's preeminent noir cinematographer Nick Musuraca sends unbroken cross lights across the men, brightly illuminating O'Brien's face and hand and also most of Lovejoy's even though he slumps down in the seat. No shadows from the wheel or windshield are visible.

GREED SETS ITS OWN TRAPS AND ENCOURAGES NOIR CHARACTERS TO ACT WITHOUT caution. Zeena (Joan Blondell) and Stanton Carlisle (Tyrone Power) in Nightmare Alley (1947) are carny hustlers whose lack of morals and abundance of native talent guarantee them at least a chance at the brass ring. But their recklessness ultimately brings them back to the depths of carny life. As they drive through the night in the almost pure black interior of a truck cab, both are marked by deep black shadows, which cut across their figures to externalize the defects in their moral make-up and act as omens of their ultimate failure. Even though Stanton has the boyish good looks and a calm mien, his set features also match a ruthless determination. The black shape of the steering wheel across his chest is like a dark anchor dragging him down. Zeena, slouched in her seat and checking her heavy make-up in a compact mirror, seems aloof and resigned. A shadowy black river has already swallowed her hand and part of her face, its vector seeming to flow forward and away as her downcast eyes follow its dark course

For Eddie Rice (John Payne), an amnesiac war veteran who returns to learn that he used to be the criminal Eddie Ricardi, the car is a deadly trap in The Crooked Way (1949). Behind the wheel is the body of Lt. Williams (Rhys Williams) who was helping Rice/Ricardi to come to grips with his past. Set up by his ex-partner, Rice suddenly confronts the reality of what he was and to what end he may now come. John Alton's unerring noir technique crystallizes the moment. A single source light hits the dead man's face, glinting off the side window and picking up the bullet hole. The light glances off his shoulder and hits Rice, jaw set, starched collar and neatly knotted tie incongruously decorous touches at a death scene, as he ponders this obvious set-up. The same light spills down over the steering wheel to pick up finger tips, the speckled gear shift knob, the cigarette in Rice's hand. On the rear window, a single streak of light barely pierces the darkness, and the upholstered roof looms over Rice's shoulder like the velvet lining of a coffin.

Sitting in an even grimmer sarcophagus are Noll Turner (Kirk Douglas) and Frankie Madison (Burt Lancaster) as they wait in the cab of their bootleggers' truck in I Walk Alone (1948). This time the light comes from below, unnaturally bright if from the dashboard but too low to be from outside. What this lighting distortion permits is a shadowy distortion of both figures that reveals their inner selves. With the dark barrel of a gun protruding from a gloved hand and a mis-shapen head behind him, Turner's face is cut by the light so that a part of his left cheek is missing. His determined gaze is appropriate to a defaced man who will abandon his partner and friend. Madison's black-jacketed trunk is hard to distinguish, one gloved hand barely visible holding the wheel, another hidden entirely. Only his face is lit and that is neatly bisected by a shadow from the wheel. He is a man doomed, about to be betrayed, the dark slash across his face anticipating the prison bars that will soon enclose him.

CHAPTER THREE

DEADLY IS THE FEMALE

LILY CARVER (GABY ROGERS) IN *KISS ME DEADLY* (1955) STRIKES A classic femme fatale pose. She is menacing and enticing at many levels. She reclines on a bed, invitingly positioned, her left hand on her hip, luring both the out-of-frame character as well as the audience towards her. The dreamy look, mouth slightly open, eyes unfocused, adds to the erotic quality. The bathrobe suggests that she wears nothing underneath, which echoes the film's first sequence in which the protagonist picked up a female hitchhiker wearing only a trench coat. The shiny revolver she holds, pointing off frame, represents a second, more obvious threat. She has taken the male icon, the gun, and made it her own. The possession of this stainless-steel phallic symbol complements the androgynous aspect of her short-cropped hair. The bars of the bedpost and the shadow on the wall and the two rows of ovals on the curtains to her left add a jagged background geometry. For a lesser man, this aura might be overpowering. For *Kiss Me Deadly*'s sneering Mike Hammer, it's just a dame with a gun.

MOTIF

Sexual Debasement

T HE THEME OF SEXUAL DEBASEMENT IS A COMMON EXPRESSIONISTIC MOTIF, EVIDENCE OF A debt to a *fin de siècle* Romanticism. In the expressionistic ethos this theme often takes the form of a femme fatale whose charms ensnare a reputable member of the bourgeoisie and frequently reduce him to acts of public humiliation. One could, of course, read in this the conventional moral of the "wages of sin," but at the same time it is quite consistent with the expressionistic interest in heightened emotional states associated with both the libido and guilt. The first example here is taken from the American edition of Hanns Heinz Ewers' *Alraune* (John Day, 1929), illustrated by Mahlon Blaine. In this illustration (figure 1), the heartless, vampiric woman Alraune "conquers" a wealthy state official. Less heartless but equally destructive is Frank Wedekind's *Lulu*. In the accompanying frame (figure 2) from Pabst's film *Pandora's Box* (1928), Lulu (portrayed by Louise Brooks) can be seen having triumphantly maneuvered Dr. Peter Schoen (Fritz Kortner) into a compromising situation before the eyes of his son and his fiancèe.

Figure 1

Figure 2

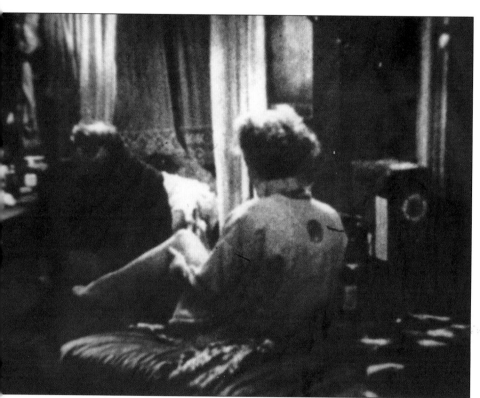

Figure 3   Figure 4

JOSEF VON STERNBERG'S *THE BLUE ANGEL* (1930)—A FILM THAT MARKS THE VERY END OF Expressionism in Germany and the beginning of the proto-noir style in the United States— best crystallizes the femme fatale character. In figure 3 Lola (Marlene Dietrich) allows the fallen Professor Rath (Emil Jannings) to put on her silk stockings for her. In a conscious homage to this scene (figure 4), German èmigrè director Fritz Lang places shy protagonist Chris Cross (Edward G. Robinson) in *Scarlet Street* (1945) at the feet of his "dominatrix" (Joan Bennett), painting her toenails in an act of submission. The ritualistic overtones of such acts of debasement suggest the coincidence of Freudianism, Expressionism, and film noir in their conjunction of sex, sadism, and fetish.   —ROBERT PORFIRIO

PEARL (JENNIFER JONES) FROM *DUEL IN THE SUN* (1946) RISES FROM HER RECLINING position wrapped in a blanket, recalling classic paintings of odalisques. Her look is less threatening and more erotic than Lily Carver's in *Kiss Me Deadly*. Her bare right shoulder is highlighted while her bare leg and thigh is obscured. Her shoulder-length soft curls contrast with Lily's cropped look, making her more traditionally feminine in appearance. The multi-colored blanket, her wild hair, and bare shoulder, leg, and feet also mark her as a "primitive," which keys her threatening aspect. The maid (Butterfly McQueen) in the foreground narrows the space in the frame and serves to focus the eye of the spectator even more emphatically on Pearl. She faces Pearl and carries the source of light which illuminates Pearl near the image center and leaves the rest of the room in shadows.

ELSA BANNISTER (RITA HAYWORTH) IN *THE LADY FROM SHANGHAI* (1948) IS A MORE ambiguous femme fatale. The spectator sees her as the narrator does, at least initially, a victim of her crippled husband's suspicious and corrupt nature. Elsa reclines on a chaise lounge in the foreground. She is dressed in white, implying innocence. Her expression is sad and meditative, staring out of frame. Like Pearl her shorter hair frames her face in a crown of soft blonde curls. Like Lily, her mouth is slightly open, the slit of bare skin, a sharp vertical perpendicular to the line of her shoulder pads, and leg exposed to just above the knee, complete an equally erotic pose. But in contrast to Lily or Pearl, Elsa is obviously of another socio-economic class. Her finely tailored clothing, large bracelets, and formidable gold wedding band mark her as a woman of means. Her husband (Everett Sloane) sits in a hammock next to her. Unlike Elsa his figure is cut in half by shadows and the webbing of the hammock, making him seem like half a man. His emasculated gaze is hard and focused on Elsa who is mentally elsewhere, not with him.

PHYLLIS DIETRICHSON (BARBARA STANWYCK) IN *DOUBLE INDEMNITY* (1944) is playful and threatening at the same time. She reclines comfortably in an armchair. She smiles and indicates no stress or tension in her face. Her arms are extended on each side of the chair as if inviting an embrace. From one hand a cigarette dangles. Her left foot juts out stiffly towards Walter Neff (Fred MacMurray). On it is a "honey of an anklet" made of fine gold. While Phyllis is in white and fully lit, Walter is in shadows, lessening his visual position in the shot, perched on the edge (literally) of an upholstered arm and (figuratively) of disaster. Although cut ominously by venetian blind shadows, even the wall behind him is brighter. His expression is one of surprise as he touches the extended limb. The dynamics of their relationship is summed up in this pose. Phyllis continually challenges the cynical Walter who, fascinated by her hard edge and overt eroticism, agrees to follow her down the road to murder and betrayal. Their kinship is expressed in the matching dangling cigarettes, hers in her left hand, his in his right.

Laura Hunt (Gene Tierney) in *Laura* (1944) is a femme fatale, or at least perceived as one both by Detective Mark McPherson (Dana Andrews) and by the real villain of the piece Waldo Lydecker (Clifton Webb). In this shot McPherson—who was obsessed with Laura's ethereal beauty when he thought she was dead but is too bitter and cynical to believe her story—grills her. Laura's face is washed out by the interrogation lamp in the foreground. Her expression is sullen and hurt as she glares at McPherson. McPherson dominates her by his superior position in the frame, sitting on the desk and bent down towards her. His clenched left fist on the desk adds to his aspect of dominance and threat. The uniformed policeman on the right acts like a dark impersonal wall, hemming Laura in, trapping her between his bulk, against which her chair is backed up, and McPherson. The interrogation lamp blocks her forward movement as its foreground presence obliterates her right shoulder and, in the two dimensions of the shot, pins her to the chair. The dimly lit wall with the vertical grid from the heater completes her visual enclosure and the claustrophobic dynamic.

RS. PARADINE (ALIDA VALLI), THE ACCUSED MURDERESS
in Alfred Hitchcock's *The Paradine Case* (1947), is not
the first object of attention in this very formalistic
composition. The three figures on the right and the two
figures on the left form a sort of short-sided triangle
which points to the prison matron (Rose McQuoid) in the background against the wall. In addition, the primary light source is
focused on her in a diagonal shaft, leaving the other figures
in shadows except for key lights on their faces. What draws the
spectator to the femme fatale, Mrs. Paradine, is the severe gazes of
the matron, the presiding officer (Gilbert Allen) sitting at the table,
his assistant (Lester Matthews) and her attorney, Sir Simon Flaquer
(Charles Coburn) to her left. All are focused on her figure at
the right center of the frame. A black column marked with height
indicators and the dark bulk of Flaquer, behind and to her left,
create a narrow visual space in which Mrs. Paradine stands upright
and resolute. In the right foreground, another man (Patrick Aherne)
holds his hat and looks off disinterestedly but the line of his arm
and glint of his hand are aimed at Mrs. Paradine. Her beauty is
highlighted by the key light shining on her forehead, face, and her
perfect profile. Her expression is somber like the other figures in the
frame. The tight bun of her hair adds an aspect of tension. As with
Laura, interrogators hem in a beautiful female figure as they try to
fathom her guilt or innocence. Both become archetypes of an
enigmatic woman, the object of the (predominantly) male gaze.

THE NAME "GILDA" FROM THE 1946 MOVIE OF THE SAME NAME EVOKES for many the epitome of the noir's femme fatale. She is a true enigma, taunting men to destruction while seeming to return their love. In this shot Gilda (Rita Hayworth) is positioned between two men in dark suits, the one closest to her is her date, Gabe (Robert Scott), the other pressed against the far wall is her tormented ex-lover Johnny Farrell (Glenn Ford). The positions of the two men express their emotional relationship to Gilda. Gabe is closer in distance and more comfortably pressing up behind her. His open expression radiates good-naturedness. Johnny, on the other hand, is separated by distance and an elaborate gate from his object of desire. He is clearly distraught as he leans against the wall for support with his body cut off by the edge of the frame. Gilda, dressed in a glittering coat which adds to her luster, gazes at Johnny with equanimity, seeming to be puzzled by his suffering. Her hands are on the gate, an impenetrable barrier between herself and Johnny's masochistic figure, as if she is undecided about whether to step behind it or to take pity on him.

RITA HAYWORTH (PLAYING CHRIS EMERY) SOFTENED HER FEMME FATALE image for *Affair in Trinidad* (1952). However, much of the same iconography appears on and around her to stamp her as a fatal woman. In this specially posed shot, she has positioned herself in an elaborate setting which typifies the style of her appearance in numerous noir films. The staircase she descends is crisscrossed with shadows, striped ropes, and other ornamentation. In fact, it resembles a spider's web, with Hayworth, the prototypical spider woman emerging from the center. She casts an ominous shadow on the wall to her right, a distorted silhouette which further enhances the feeling of threat and doom. Her pose is regal as she places her left hand on the banister and throws her bare shoulders back, as if consciously waiting for the portrait to be taken. Her scarf precedes her like the train of a bride. Even the background decor, the entwined figures on the wall painting behind her and the primitive dancing woman that forms the base of the lamp at right, mesh with the understated themes of eroticism and feminine control.

N THIS SHOT FROM *THE WOMAN IN THE WINDOW* (1945), ART combines with reality to form a compelling modernistic triptych. Alice Reed (Joan Bennett) stands frame left, a striking figure in black, her facial features softly highlighted and the black edges of her feathered hat cutting into her forehead while dots of light glint off her beaded jacket. To the right of the frame is a rendition of her image by an artist. It is a softer version of the woman. Her hair is longer and her expression more vulnerable, but the pose in the painting is a rough mirror of Alice on the left. The painting is also key lit. In addition there is a slight reflection of Alice in the window to the right of the head of the woman in the painting. This visual layering makes Alice seem even more mysterious. The line between reality and fantasy is blurred in this shot, as it is in the mind of the off-frame protagonist, who stopped to look at the painting only to have the actual woman appear. The fatality in this psychological noir, where dream states are a key to the narrative, is in the mind of the beholder.

THE THREAT POSED BY ANNIE LAURIE STARR (PEGGY CUMMINS) IN *Gun Crazy* (1950) is much more dynamic and violent than Gilda or even Lily Carver. In this shot her husband and co-conspirator, Bart Tare (John Dall), has a difficult time restraining Annie in her violent desires. Confined to the left side of the frame Annie pushes forth, gun in hand, as Bart wraps his arm around her, pulling her back. Both are united by costuming, wearing overcoats and dark glasses but separated by dynamic motion. Hers is to the right of the frame, towards the open space of the street while his movement is to the left of frame away from the scene of the crime and the danger. Annie is the dominant one in the relationship from the beginning, instigating the action. In a film originally titled "Deadly is the Female," Bart is a reactive character, leading to a sexual role reversal implicit in the theme of the film, in which he is more sexually and criminally modest. Bart's perception of the relationship, that they "go together, I don't know how, maybe like guns and ammunition," is stylistically supported from their first meeting at a carnival side show trick-shooting exhibition. And Annie's association of crime and guns with sexual arousal is as explicit as Bart's is covert. When he restrains Annie, the gun speaks of violence, her expression speaks of sex, and both psychological components are in play.

THE *STRANGE LOVE OF MARTHA IVERS* (1946) PRESENTS A YOUNGER VERSION OF THE femme fatale: Janis Wilson portrays Martha as a teenager. (Barbara Stanwyck is the adult version.) Here she threatens her mother (Judith Anderson). The dynamics of the poses reveal all. Martha, to the left of the frame, is reaching for her mother's neck as Mr. O'Neil (Roman Bohnen) in the center restrains her. Mrs. Ivers is stiff and impassive. She shows no fear, while Martha's expression is trancelike, almost demented. While locked in the same two dimensional plane and merged together through their black costumes, O'Neil is, in those same two dimensions at least, between them, almost like two boxers and a referee. His face registers strain and tension as the diagonal thrust of his arm attempts to cut the flow of the movement from left to right, from Martha to her mother. Although Mrs. Ivers is taller and O'Neil is trapped between them, the young Martha is the dynamic vortex of the shot.

EVEN WHEN POSED ALONE, THE FEMME FATALE OFTEN INTERACTS WITH AN OFF-SCREEN protagonist. In some situations, the pose is purely archetypal. As in the pose from *Affair in Trinidad*, Rita Hayworth, in *Gilda*, can single-handedly evoke the composite allure and menace of the femme fatale. In *Gilda* Hayworth's performance of "Put the Blame on Mame" sets the standard for the noir sultry songstress. With the background barely visible behind her, all attention is focused as she occupies center stage. Her actions imply total lack of inhibition. Her shiny black dress clings to her curves, exposing her bare shoulders and threatening to bare her torso. Her mouth is open and her luxurious hair tumbles over her shoulders. She grasps the elbow-length glove she has just removed from her right arm above her head, forming a circle which draws attention to her upthrust face. The black of her costume and the paleness of her skin also are calculated to create an erotic contrast.

JULIE BENSON (JANE RUSSELL) IN JOSEF VON STERNBERG'S MACAO (1952) ALSO occupies center stage but with less authority as the musicians around her diffuse the spectator's focus. The large black bass fiddle to her right is particularly distracting. She also lacks the dynamic contrast in costuming which Hayworth possessed as Gilda. Julie's costume is white rather than black, blending in with her skin. The lines of the dress are smooth and without highlight or luster. The draped bodice flattens rather than enhances her bustline. Her arms are up like Hayworth's but the dress does not seem to slip down. While Hayworth's simple necklace mirrors the curve of her upper lip, Russell's is too elaborate and heavy. The erotic touches are subtle: her mouth is open suggesting a lack of inhibition and the dark clarinets strike a quasi-phallic pose, possibly a wry touch from von Sternberg; but overall the shot lacks the pure "animal magnetism" of Gilda.

Fran Page (Gloria Grahame) in *Song of the Thin Man* (1947) recedes into the group. In the longer shot, her figure cannot dominate the composition in the manner of Gilda or Julie Benson, but her expression and her pose are also less inviting and open. She seems to lean on the piano for support and her face is sullen and suspicious. The black of her costume does not set her apart but forces her to blend in with the dark suits of the orchestra members. She is the center of the composition simply because she is standing while the orchestra sits and because the instruments of the band members point towards her as they form a semi-circle around her. Her bare white shoulders and her blonde hair also set her off from the darkness and gloom around her.

I N "THE GIRL HUNT BALLET" FROM VINCENTE MINNELLI'S FILM VERSION OF THE BAND WAGON (1953) Cyd Charisse plays a dual role. Here Fred Astaire as the detective and Cyd Charisse as the elusive and dangerous object of his search spin in opposite directions and eye each other suspiciously over their shoulders. Their conflict is externalized through pose and costuming. As the staging and costuming are conscious parodies of the noir treatment of the femme fatale, her cutaway black-sequined gown, long gloves and necklace seem almost restrained as do his white suit and dark shirt. In reversal of the stereotype, the sequence ends with the revelation that the blonde is the villain and the brunette, the "good" girl.

A MORE CLASSIC SORT OF SATIRE IS AT PLAY IN *SUNSET BOULEVARD* (1950). As class divisions are often crucial in identifying femme fatales, Norma Desmond (Gloria Swanson) is a wealthy, forgotten silent film star who is surrounded by her possessions. As they sit on a sofa during a private soiree, a small orchestra plays behind them. Surrounding her are objects of the past (her photographs, jewelry, and gown) and one of the present (her lover Joe Gillis, played by William Holden). Her bare shoulder, necklace, bracelets, dark curls, mouth slightly open, even the wire holder on her left index finger—all are caricatures of the classic fatal woman of film noir. Norma reclines, her legs stretched onto Joe's lap and her right arm extended as if encompassing the world around her—a classic femme fatale pose. If her relaxed posture implies a queenly ease, Joe Gillis is, on the other hand, uncomfortable in this world. He clutches his arms around his waist as if to protect himself and his expression is downcast. His head is flanked by pictures of a young Norma, fencing him in, while Norma's legs on his lap perform the same function as does the pillow on the right edge of the frame. At the left, a champagne bucket could wryly connote a captive phallus. Joe also seems very uncomfortable in his "monkey suit." He is very much the fly caught in Norma's Gothic web.

CHARLIE DAVIS (JOHN GARFIELD) HAS A LOOK OF SENSUAL PLEASURE IN *BODY AND SOUL* (1947) as Alice (Hazel Brooks) loosens his tie, in preparation for further physical and psychological manipulations. Her position in the frame, like that of Norma Desmond, is dominant. She leans over Charlie's reclining figure, effectively pinning him down, although unlike Joe Gillis, Charlie has no desire to leave. In addition, her garb and make-up signify her status as a spider woman. Her black evening dress and dark tresses drape off her bare, white shoulders while a kicklight lightens the hair on top of her head. An insect-like brooch is strategically placed in her cleavage. Her deep red lipstick and her high, thinly drawn eyebrows give her face a more predatory aspect. Alice represents the life of money and corruption that proletarian boxer Charlie has just entered. She also serves as a foil to his working class girlfriend back home.

BRIGID O'SHAUGNESSY (MARY ASTOR) IN *THE MALTESE FALCON* (1941) indicates her social standing by her costume and appearance. She wears fur draped over her shoulders and a tasteful hat crowns her carefully coifed wavy hair. Even the casual spread fingers of her left hand reveal nails that are impeccably manicured. Her dominance in the frame is indicated by her superior height relative to Sam Spade (Humphrey Bogart) and to the sitting secretary (Lee Patrick). She also dominates as the gaze of both the secretary and Spade are directed at her at the right of the frame. While Brigid's expression is friendly and her open-mouthed smile is mirrored by the secretary's more discreet one, it is Spade's gaze which is telling. Mouth slightly open, eyes slightly sidecast, the look is at once anticipatory and apprehensive, an appropriate introductory dynamic to a relationship in which she will lead him through a labyrinth of lies. While Brigid and Spade stand quite close to each other they do not touch or even blend in the two dimensions of the frame. He stands stiffly, with his hand thrust in his pocket forming a vector at the elbow that seems to push her away. The table and the shadow of the letters on the wall between and behind Spade and Brigid are also subtle barriers that anticipate the mistrust between them.

VELMA/MRS. GRAYLE (CLAIRE TREVOR) IN *MURDER MY SWEET* (1944) is a social climber who has hidden her tawdry, lower class background. Her dual identities as the tartish Velma and the upper crust Mrs. Grayle are captured in this composition. Surrounded by her spacious mansion, she is, like Brigid O'Shaugnessy, tastefully coifed as her carefully manicured hand grasps Philip Marlowe's (Dick Powell). However, her social background emerges in the gaudy bracelet, the bare midriff and her aggressive look. While that seductive, upward gaze, as she bends to Marlowe's lighter does not belie her current status, it exacerbates Marlowe's suspicions. He assumes the classic pose of the detective when confronted with a femme fatale. He examines her closely and suspiciously. He dominates her in positioning because of his height and the black of his suit in relation to her white outfit, but her two-handed grasp of his single hand demonstrates the power she possesses.

ANOTHER SOCIAL CLIMBER IS BELLE ADAIR (PEGGY CUMMINS) SEEN HERE IN *Moss Rose* (1947). Serenely beautiful in her Victorian wrap and silk scarf, Belle lives up to her name. Her impassive countenance increases her enigmatic status as her suitor, Sir Alexander Sterling (Victor Mature), tries to permeate her facade with his piercing gaze. Both are locked in a rectangular block of light, a wedge that holds them as firmly as their interlocking fates. Belle is accused of blackmail and general unscrupulousness while Sterling's morals are never clear until the resolution of the film. As they pose full face against profile neither seems comfortable. Sterling's hat and overcoat connect him to the black surroundings as he tilts forward. Belle's white feathery wrap and medium-gray scarf act as a contrast to that blackness. Sterling's profile is outlined by his own shadow which reaches out and touches Belle. More than anything the severe line at the top creates a sense of being boxed in, as in the interrogation scene in *Laura*. For Belle, though, pinned into the corner by Sterling's dark bulk that sense is even more acute.

POPPY (GENE TIERNEY, LEFT) IN *THE SHANGHAI GESTURE* (1941) IS A FEMME FATALE ON the way down the social ladder. Her involvement with Mother Gin Sling (Ona Munson) leads this daughter of a diplomat into a life of gambling, drugs and sex, events made even more disturbing by the fact that Mother Gin Sling is her real mother. Poppy's descent into corruption is revealed by her slatternly pose, as she sits on a bar top with a cigarette dangling from her mouth. She is slouched over and her eyes are half-closed as if in a trance. Her right hand grasps tensely at her right knee. The source of the tension may be her mother's grasp of Poppy's other hand. Mother Gin Sling is the second femme fatale in this composition and by far the more powerful of the two. Although Poppy has more bulk in the frame, the way Mother Gin Sling holds her daughter's hand indicates her power. Her straightforward expression and pose imply strength while her black dress full of glinting highlights and oriental headdress give her visual dominance. Her extreme make-up, including the arching eyebrows and thin lips, also adds to her sinister appearance.

Candy (Jean Peters, left) in *Pickup on South Street* (1953) is a proletarian femme fatale, who uses her charms to survive. Her heavy make-up, cheap bracelet, pin, and earrings, and her arm cocked on her hip—all are indicators of her class. The tie in the foreground represents the many men in her life as she stares at it disdainfully. Moe (Thelma Ritter) proffers the tie to her suspiciously, her gesture making the symbolic item the central point of the frame. The shabby decor of the room also types both Candy and Moe as offspring of the working class. The tired and worn Moe with her thin, tawdry robe and aging face represents both a maternal image and a possible mirror to Candy's future, if she continues in the life she has cut out for herself. While Candy is taller and closer to the foreground giving her more physical dimension than Moe, the older woman's forceful gaze and the light in her eyes reveal her resilience.

CORA SMITH (LANA TURNER) IN *THE POSTMAN ALWAYS RINGS TWICE* (1946) COMPLETELY dominates this frame. She is positioned in her white waitress outfit between her husband, Nick Smith (Cecil Kellaway, right), and her lover, Frank Chambers (John Garfield), who are both dressed in dark suits. The primary light—the ostensible source is the table lamp—is on her, also increasing her importance in the frame. As she clears the table, she watches apprehensively. In this shot, she is both the literal and figurative apex of the love triangle, and so must watch her every move and each change of mood on the part of her lover or her husband. The respective right hands of the two men are outstretched towards each other as if in a tentative challenge. Nick's face registers anger and confusion, while Frank remains concerned but calm. The roadside cafe with its oilcloth, checkered tablecloths sets the milieu as working class, reinforced by her waitress garb and Frank's rumpled collar. But the hairstyle and halo of blonde hair separate Cora from this milieu.

THE DOOMED WAITRESS STELLA (LINDA DARNELL) IN *FALLEN ANGEL* (1946) serves coffee to the unassuming man who will eventually murder her, Mark Judd (Charles Bickford). There are several unsettling design elements in this composition which set a foreboding tone. The shot is criss-crossed with several sets of bars. In the background the slits of the venetian blinds form horizontal bars while Stella's uniform contrasts with verticals stripes. Finally in the foreground at the right edge of the frame there are a series of vertical bars from a countertop juke box selector which cuts into her left shoulder. While these horizontal lines hem Stella in, the slick counter top forms a pool of light across which their gray arms seem to meet and merge somewhere behind the clutter of dispensers, so that the murderer and eventual victim are conjoined. Stella looks down from her superior position—she stands while he sits—with an arrogant but sensual expression. Judd does not look up as if afraid to engage her gaze while the coffee pot hovers near frame center. Like many proletarian femme fatales, Stella is doomed. That doom is both individual and cultural for the patriarchal society of noir's classic period repressed the women whose behavior violated its mores.

I N *THE BIG HEAT* (1953), DETECTIVE DAVE O'BANNION'S (GLENN Ford) relentless pursuit of the mobsters who killed his wife has involved disaffected moll Debby Marsh (Gloria Grahame), now disfigured after being scalded by her angry boyfriend. Driven by her own desire for revenge, Debby will eventually commit murder before being fatally shot herself. In Fritz Lang's fatalistic world view, molls, strippers, and hookers, social outcasts like Debby, are beyond salvation: in trying to help O'Bannion she dooms herself. Hiding out in a hotel room, she sits impassively, neck and right eye bandaged, face shadowed by the window light. Visually separated from her by the curtain running vertically down the center of the frame, O'Bannion glances back from the window, the highlights on his brow and cheek mirroring her white bandages. O'Bannion seems uncertain; but, while her look is non-committal, Debby has decided on a course as severe and relentless as his.

CHAPTER FOUR

THE DARK MIRROR

Many commentators have considered the psychology of the prototypical noir character. Certainly, the influence of psychology as the preeminent method for the explanation of unusual and even aberrant behaviors could not be overlooked by the post-war noir filmmakers. To depict their noir characters, so often haunted by a dark past, by deep psychological scars which lead to obsessive/ neurotic even psychotic behavior, their imagery was often rife with overt Freudian symbols. While most of these protagonists are men, often disturbed veterans of World War II, many women also gazed into film noir's dark mirror.

A VARIANT SPLIT PERSONALITY IS FEATURED IN BILLY WILDER'S *SUNSET BOULEVARD* (1950). IN THE WELL-known final scene, Max Von Mayerling (Erich von Stroheim) watches sternly over his former star, Norma Desmond (Gloria Swanson), as she enters completely and irrevocably into her world of movie star fantasy while police and reporters watch on. The schizophrenic Norma's descent into her own personal dark past is indicated by her expression, make-up, and costume. Norma is dressed in a 1920s-style gown which flows off her aging body. The contrast with the young Norma, who was a star, has been repeatedly established in previous scenes. Now having killed her faithless young lover, the middle-aged Norma wears the mask of her young self with make-up and clothing from the period of her youth and stardom. It is extreme, almost expressionistic. Her distorted mien exemplifies her dementia in a way that mimics both the rictus of the hopelessly insane and the affectations of silent film performances. Norma's awareness of the throng around her, staring at her, is dimmed like an actor in performance. Since Norma acts out her own fantasy script, she sees the press cameras before her, out of frame, as the reenactment of sound stage she visited earlier in the film. The dynamic of the shot effectively aligns with Norma's "direction" as the line of the stairway behind her and the line of human bodies both trace a trajectory towards her, making Norma the emotional as well as dynamic center of the composition.

SPLIT PERSONALITY IS EXTERNALIZED IN ROBERT SIODMAK'S *THE DARK MIRROR* (1946) by the use of twin protagonists. Ruth Collins comforts her "evil" twin sister Terry (both parts played by Olivia De Havilland, with Amelita Ward acting as photo double in angles such as this) while Detective Stevenson (Thomas Mitchell) examines them suspiciously. Ruth is the "good sister" and so her expression is one of concern tinged with sadness and a degree of resolve. She only seems the stronger figure, as Terry is the aggressive and unscrupulous personality. The ostensibly dominant figure in this shot is the detective, who stands, towering over the sisters with his stern expression, the tightly wrapped black coat giving him a monolithic bulk. As the sisters huddle together the lines of their garments and curve of their shoulders merge, giving them, together, a physical mass which might resist that of Stevenson and the ordered world which he represents. The mirror on the wall is another obvious symbol of duality. The small table lamp which acts as a source light separates the suspicious detective from the schizophrenic duo in the two dimensions of the frame.

OTHER FEMALE PROTAGONISTS ARE VICTIMS OF PSYCHOLOGICAL MANIPULATION. Leslie (Merle Oberon, right background) in *Dark Waters* (1944) is scarred by the death of her parents but soon becomes the victim of dear ones around her. Uncle Norbert (John Qualen) dominates the image as he stands in the foreground to the right of the frame. His angry, suspicious eyes dart to the left of the frame, carefully listening to the conversation of Leslie and Aunt Emily (Fay Bainter, left background). As one of the plotters against her sanity Nobert has helped frame Leslie as securely as the square of the draperies around her at the edge of the bed. The ominous patterns of light behind Leslie on the well, thrown by the bed curtains, also unsettle the spectator and mark Leslie as the real center of attention rather than the shadowy, more prominent figure of Norbert in the foreground.

KIT (JOHN GARFIELD, RIGHT) IN *THE FALLEN SPARROW* (1943) confronts his own demons in the form of Dr. Skass (Walter Slezak), a Nazi who was involved in Kit's torture during the Spanish Civil War. Kit's figure is diminutive in the frame, particularly when compared with Dr. Skass's hulking, black silhouette in the foreground center. The psychological scars are visible in Kit's expression as well as in his position seeking solace behind the globe and the armchair in the right corner of the frame. Everything in the frame seems threatening to his small figure: the single light source at the left of the frame creating the ominous shadows, the huge arches towering above his head, even the drapery and ropes hanging above and to Kit's right.

I N *MOONRISE* (1949) DANNY HAWKINS (DANE CLARK) IS HIS OWN tormentor. Even though he is comforted and supported by his girl, Gilly (Gail Russell), he cannot overcome his belief that he has "bad blood." As they stand in a forest, an emblem of the primeval, the key light on their faces from a single off-screen source leaves the rest of the frame in relative darkness. They look back, figuratively, towards the ghosts which haunt Danny, his profile expression is tinged with uncertainty, hopeful but apprehensive, while Gilly's fuller-faced and wide-eyed innocence seems ready to confront the demons. The strong kicks of light on her shoulder, cheek, and forehead at frame center dominate, and the light on his face is a dimmer reflection, in line with her stronger emotional position and his need for her support.

A LLIDA (HEDY LAMARR) IN *EXPERIMENT PERILOUS* (1944) SEEKS SOLACE FROM her knight in black armor, Dr. Bailey (George Brent), against her domineering husband who has purposely turned a vibrant, beautiful woman into a neurotic weakling. This intimate composition in black and white unites the two lovers in shadow and light and in the black of their costumes but opposes them in pose and expression. Allida bends her head in submission towards the man she believes might save her. Her expression is one of contented resignation. She is made to look even more vulnerable by her veil and the soft fur on her shoulders. Bailey's pose is upright and strong. He bends his head only slightly towards her with an expression of concern mixed with a certain hesitancy. As in *Moss Rose*, source light from outside the carriage creates a hard shadow line behind them. Unlike those two figures, the intimate pose of these characters defines a different relationship and underscores the psychological dependency.

THIS SHOT FROM *GASLIGHT* (1944), ANOTHER PERIOD NOIR ABOUT a husband intentionally tormenting his wife, captures the persecutor-husband in the act. Gregory Anton (Charles Boyer) adjusts the gas lamp on the left side of the frame, the flame lighting his face and revealing a look of intensity, even dementia. His right arm cuts the frame to create a dynamic movement to the lamp and back to his face. There is a claustrophobic dimension to this image caused by the ceiling above, the ladder on the right side of the frame which cuts into his head, while the bar and his arm create an enclosed wedge around the perpetrator. Even though he is the victimizer, the image implies that he may be trapped by his own obsessions and neuroses. Equally significant is the array of straight lines at odd angles and in different shades of gray—ceiling, amp pipe, ladder, rung, cane, arm, coat stripes, hat, and painting below his elbow—creating a maze around his transfixed gaze at frame center.

I N FRITZ LANG'S SECRET BEYOND THE DOOR (1948), MARK LAMPHERE (MICHAEL Redrgrave) is haunted by the murder of his wife and the murderous impulses he feels towards his new wife Celia (Joan Bennett). Mark dominates the frame with his superior height and by the dynamic motion of winding the scarf around his right hand. Celia's head is thrown back in fear, but she looks at Lamphere with concern as well as apprehension. There is a hidden strength in her eyes and her posture, her well-lit shoulders thrust forward to catch the shadow of the scarf, as she is determined to lead her husband out of this morass of guilt and psychoses. Even the shadow of the scarf on her throat and shoulders does not soften her resolve. The gray background lacks the shadowy photography more typical of the noir style, trading it instead for a more mundane array that does not set off the foreground figures. Lang often used a higher key to create a sense of everyday determinism which linked the characters to the surroundings.

THE TENSION AND SENSE OF MENACE IN *SUDDEN FEAR* (1952) IS unmistakable. The love-hate relationship between husband (Lester portrayed by Jack Palance) and wife (Myra, Joan Crawford) creates suspicion and threat at every turn. Lester seems to dominate this shot. His large figure blocks the doorway as well as Myra's movement forward. The normal lens aperture and focal length limits the focal plane blurring his foreground mass and slightly foreshortening the distance to the wall behind her. Lester's left hand is poised on the edge of the door so that he further encloses her with the dark aspect of his body in the two dimensions of the frame. In this context, the small bright glint off his wedding band stands out ominously. Above her head a gray line of wainscoting runs from each edge of the doorway completely boxing her in. Counterbalancing this and sustaining visual tension, the light centers on Myra's surprised and possibly frightened expression and, in the room behind her, creates a very bright spot above her shoulders that seems to burst out from her white collar. While Lester's form fills much more of the frame, Myra's presence is much brighter reinforcing the fact that she is menaced by Lester but not necessarily afraid. The highlights on his shoulder, arm, and hand seem to bounce from her face and hold him back. A horizontal bar of light subtly crosses her face below the eyes creating a visual split echoed in the vertical division down Lester's back. This split visually suggests each character's undecided emotional state as well as their divided feelings towards each other.

LIKE LESTER IN *SUDDEN FEAR*, LEWT (GREGORY PECK) IN DAVID O. SELZNICK'S production *Duel in the Sun* (1946) dominates the frame with his shadowy figure, his back to the viewer. He blocks his lover Pearl's (Jennifer Jones) forward movement as she is pushed into a corner. Pearl seems vulnerable by her inferior size and because all exits seem blocked. Her right palm presses against the wall for support. There is also a bruise on her right cheek which indicates that there has been violence before. A deep shadow also crosses the right side of her face, possibly cast by Lewt. Despite being hemmed in by the walls and Lewt, the key light makes her the visual center. Pearl's eyes show defiance more than fear. The mouth slightly open and the fixed gaze are even erotic, which is in keeping with the sado-masochistic nature of a relationship which will end when they shoot each other.

ALAN (JOSEPH COTTEN) AND VICTORIA (JENNIFER JONES) FROM *LOVE LETTERS* (1945) are another couple caught in a web of deceit and mental illness tied to her amnesia. While the couple struggle to resolve the missing past, it looms like an unseen reflection. As they sit together with a moonlit lake in the background, their physical closeness suggests that they are lovers; and yet there is an undercurrent of wariness and unease. The streak of light on the lake is narrow and surrounded by dark waters which could be emblematic of that missing past. They are not embracing but are at right angle to each other. They use the trunk of the tree on the left of the frame for support rather than each other. Alan's look is pensive and away from Victoria. Victoria's gaze is towards Alan but is also pensive rather than joyful. The half light on each face reinforces their emotional indecisiveness. Ultimately, their pose, their expressions, and even their surroundings are not as idyllic as they first appear.

I N *CAUGHT* (1949) MULTI-MILLIONAIRE SMITH OHLRIG (ROBERT RYAN) confronts his own demons in the form of paranoia, hypochondria, and alcoholism. The dramatic tension of this image is at the edges of the frame: Ohlrig on the right and a glass on the left. Smith's right arm, in fact his entire body, is stretched towards that empty glass, as if it were his salvation. The capsized champagne bottle on the right next to Ohlrig reinforces the sense of emptiness and frustration while its gilt-foil neck points to the glass. The very large mansion behind him suggests an abundance of space and that Ohrlig can buy whatever he wants. The mansion also externalizes the mental state of its disturbed owner, being full of dark recesses that mirror his paranoia and rage. The irony of Ohlrig's position in the foreground by the glass, bottle, ice bucket, and cigarette pack is that he has consumed it all and can only focus on the emptiness.

ALCOHOL ALSO FIGURES IN ANOTHER IMAGE FROM *CRY VENGEANCE* (1954). VIC (MARK STEVENS) IS literally and figuratively eating himself away with his desire for revenge. He has been jailed, mislead, and threatened but will not relent. His pose in this shot externalizes his depression. He sits huddled over, his arms forming a pillow into which he burrows like a child. He refuses to raise his eyes to the beautiful comforter above him, Peg (Martha Hyer). The bottle and glass are at center frame as they, too, represent the escape he unsuccessfully seeks. Peg sits above him on the table like an angel in white, comforting him. Her right hand holds the bottle while her left hand rests on his shoulder. Again the light which falls on the side of his face seems to bounce off her figure. Her white costume and his dark one also set up a striking contrast. The wood-plank walls behind them are plain and unadorned, adding to the depressing atmosphere around Vic.

POLICE SERGEANT STEVENS (LAWRENCE TIERNEY, LEFT) IN *THE FEMALE JUNGLE* (1955) battles the world around him to establish that he is not a rogue cop. His reputation as a detective is tarnished by alcoholism as well as brutality, both of which drive his self-destructive behavior. The expressions on these two men's faces reveal their desperation. Stevens's square-jawed face is hard and fierce. His right hand clutches his victim's coat. Claude Almstead (John Carradine, right) is not unexpectedly apprehensive. His grimace distorts his face so that the intensity of Stevens's look, underscored by the wedge of light on the wall behind them, seems to send shockwaves rippling through Almstead's cheek. Although both men's bodies merge at the bottom of the frame into one unbroken block of black clothing, it is their faces to which the spectator is drawn. The men's chins align and stand out against a dark shadow, so that the alternate reading is another dark mirror, as Stevens looks into a face that could be his own in years to come.

JACQUELINE GIBSON (JEAN BROOKS) IN VAL LEWTON'S *THE SEVENTH Victim* (1943) is a study in self-absorbed alienation. She is obsessed with death and the absurdity of life. Her expression is downcast while her dark eyes reveal unplumbed depths of her existential depression. Her face is side-lit (from a source off frame to the right) creating a schizophrenic quality in her image. The post to the left of the frame, against which she leans, throws a dark vertical through the shot from top to bottom and confines her to the right of the frame. Her luxurious dark hair melds with her fur giving her a purely animalistic dimension and suggesting a caged animal which is an apt metaphor for her mental state.

LT. CORNELL (RICHARD BOONE) WORSHIPS AT THE SHRINE OF HIS OBSESSION, the title character (Jean Peters) in *Vicki* (1953). His face has the apprehensive look of an acolyte who serves a deity he can never possess. His hands encircle his most recent offering of flowers for the goddess. He has arranged his altar on a wall of his apartment. A triptych of pictures of Vicki, one large one in the middle flanked by two smaller ones (the one on the left of the frame is partially obscured by the bouquet of flowers), is the centerpiece. Two lit votive-like candles flank the larger photograph in the middle. The religious overtones are none too subtle but totally appropriate when the spectator finally understands the psychosis of the worshiper. *Vicki* is a remake of *I Wake Up Screaming* (1942). In the earlier version, Laird Cregar created a wider-eyed, more effete Lt. Cornell, and Carole Landis was a more ethereal object of worship; but the effect is very much the same. *Vicki* is a proletarian version of *I Wake Up Screaming* in keeping with the shifting canvas of the noir style in the decade that separates the productions. The obsessive behavior of Boone's rough-hewn and hard-bitten Cornell is also more unexpected than it would be from an actor like Cregar.

THE DELINEATION OF THE DISTURBED COP IN *VICKI* AND THE CHAOS WHEN THOSE SWORN to uphold order behave from personal and/or obsessive motives draws as much from *Laura* (1945) as from *I Wake Up Screaming*. Although the pose is strikingly similar, Lt. Mark McPherson (Dana Andrews) is a very different character from Cornell. For Cornell worship at the shrine is a disturbing experience, more sad than exhilarating. And the object of his desire is a proletarian woman— a former waitress. All the images in *Vicki* are realistic in detail; the central one features oversized earrings that are a bit too gaudy. The foreground image is in a gilt frame which combines with the open-mouthed smile, head titled back, and a hand-through-the-hair pose to create a noir icon of an attainable female. McPherson looks at a slightly stylized painting, the features less defined by broader strokes. The hairstyle, the scarf at the neck, one arm held languidly at the side, and the halo-like light around the body are all part of an aristocratic treatment of Laura (Gene Tierney). Like Cornell, McPherson is entranced by the woman whose murder he is investigating, but his gaze is serene, transcendent, and, while his hands are at his waist like Cornell's, he bears no offering. McPherson stands further back from the painting, is less intimate with it, and physically insulates himself with his trench coat and hat.

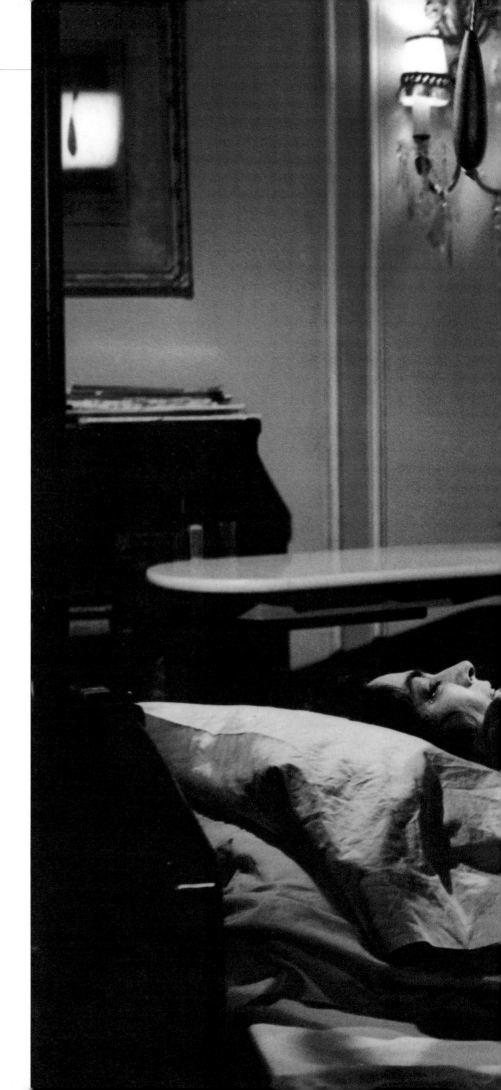

BABY JANE HUDSON (BETTE DAVIS) CHAINS UP HER SISTER BLANCHE (Joan Crawford) in Robert Aldrich's gothic *What Ever Happened to Baby Jane?* (1962). As one of the last vestiges of the classic period, the style of this film, seven years after *Kiss Me Deadly*, combines straightforward and satirical elements. Baby Jane, like Lt. Cornell and Norma Desmond, is lost in her own world. Blaming her sister for her misery she tortures her with the skill and flare of a Torquemada. Even more than with Norma Desmond in *Sunset Boulevard*, the manic behavior and make-up leave little to the imagination. Baby Jane's aging face is powdered white with dark lipstick and heavy shading on her eyes that are entirely grotesque. Her expression as she trusses up her crippled sister is one of distraction and elation, as if she is entranced by a thought or a vision somewhere off frame. Jane's laced-edged white house dress contrasts with her victim-sister's black attire creating tension through contrast even as it parodies the traditional associations of white/black, good/evil in the manner of "The Girl Hunt Ballet." The expression on Blanche's face is one of semi-conscious agony. The shadowy room also adds to the mood as do its tasteful furniture and decorations, out of keeping with the simple, cheap frocks of the sisters, implying both have survived beyond their time.

THE LOW ANGLE MAY SLIGHTLY DISORIENT THE VIEWER AND MAKE THE figures of Richard Mason (Humphrey Bogart) and Evelyn Turner (Alexis Smith) loom more dramatically. In *Conflict* (1945) Mason is willing to murder his wife in order to be with Evelyn. His figure bends over hers but not menacingly. In fact he exudes vulnerability. His expression is pained, almost pleading. His left hand on hers is a gesture of reassurance and love. His inclined posture may even be a prelude to kneeling before her. Evelyn senses his vulnerability and reacts with a smile but keeps her distance, shoulder squared back as she leans into the arm of the sofa and draws up her legs. While her face is uplifted as if to return his gaze, her eyes are looking down towards the bright white handkerchief in his breast pocket while she keeps her right hand on her lap. Her position on the couch is relaxed even sensual, but her legs are exposed to the spectator not to Mason and her angular body language is not warm, barely cordial. The use of the low angle makes the ceiling visible and creates a v-line which separates his face from hers while seeming to press down on him. All this reaffirms that the pressure to act is on him, while Evelyn may sit quietly and await the outcome.

MR. AND MRS. KELLERTON (PAUL STEWART AND RUTH ROMAN) IN THE FILM adaptation of Cornell Woolrich's *The Window* (1949) are killers whose brutality extends to children. Witnessed murdering a sailor by a young boy, the couple is determined to silence him. The trajectory of this shot is downward. Both Kellertons look suspiciously behind their left shoulders. The light is from below and to the side, a variant on what Alton called "criminal lighting," which creates dark shadows under their eyes, noses, and in the center of their brows. Thus "marked" they appear guilty as well as wary. The rails of the banister to their right foreshadow their eventual failure as does the insecurity and downward thrust of their gaze. Although Mrs. Kellerton is higher up on the stairs and therefore taller in the frame than Mr. Kellerton, he pushes towards her from below, as if holding her up. These co-conspirators are joined emotionally and physically in the shot, so much so that, if he were to reach up behind her, the hand which claws at the rail could be either hers or his.

CAPPY (JACK PALANCE, LEFT) IS A HIRED KILLER WHO THREATENS CLARE (Linda Darnell) and Russ Lambert (Robert Mitchum, right) in *Second Chance* (1953). Again the low angle, exacerbated by the tilt off vertical which is meant to render the angle of a cable car, upsets the spectator's sense of normal placement. The rope across the center of the frame further disturbs the reading of the shot as it horizontally bisects the entire image. Cappy dominates the frame as he is at the higher end of the tilt of the camera and leans back comfortably. His arm rests on his hip as he levels the gun. This menacing pose is reinforced by the shadow over his eyes. The cramped space of the tramway car also amplifies the tension, so that, in fact, Cappy's casual posture in this tense composition, with his right leg bent forward, is out of place. Clare leans towards him, while Russ, behind her, holds her arm, perhaps to restrain her, perhaps to help her balance on the uneven floor.

THIS FREEZE-FRAME FROM *NEW YORK CONFIDENTIAL* (1955) captures noir brutality in mid-act. Charlie Lupo (Broderick Crawford) is a vicious mobster who has built his career on a foundation of coercion. Even his daughter, Kathy (Anne Bancroft), is not immune from his terror. Charlie's left hand, out of focus after he swings it across his daughter's face, underscores the distortion in his features. His daughter's face, snapped to her left by the force of his blow, is frozen in a moment of pain. Yet in the clenched teeth, the squint, the upraised cheeks, and the arch of the eyebrows, the two expressions—anger and pain, parent and child, male and female, oppressor and victim— are equated by noir style and become another dark mirror.

CODY JARRETT (JAMES CAGNEY, RIGHT) IN *WHITE HEAT* (1949) IS FAR MORE DISTURBED THAN Charlie Lupo and is regarded by many as film noir's prototypical psychopath. A gangster with an Oedipal complex, Cody's physical stature and "dough boy" physique are but physical masks for a festering viciousness. In this shot he seems almost lackadaisical and passive. He leans on his right side and accepts the stronger gesture of his prison mate, Hank Fallon (Edmond O'Brien), who supports him with his right arm. Fallon has just saved Jarrett from injury, and Jarrrett gazes up at him with acceptance, almost affection, underlining the implicit homoerotic elements of the film. Fallon would normally dominate the image with his forceful gesture and his superior physique and height. Their prison garb unites them even as they blend in with the drab prison background. Building on the fact that the viewer has already witnessed the depth of Jarrett's disturbance, his body mass spread horizontally across the frame as he leans back on a workbench and the intensity of his gaze, hatless and disheveled, make Jarrett the real nexus of power and emotion in the shot.

S ALTON REMARKED, "THERE IS NOTHING ROMANTIC ABOUT THE DRAB, GRAY PRISON scene." In fact starkness of decor is an effective visual technique in many film noir. In *Black Tuesday* (1954) murderer Vincent Canelli (Edward G. Robinson) is transported by prison officials into the place of execution. Their figures are dwarfed by the drab and gray decor, stark bare walls are washed over by a naturalistic key light ostensibly from a distant off-frame window, which casts the long shadows of the four men across the floor even as the execution hood blocks the light from Canelli's left side. To the right of the frame the electric chair waits for its victim. Although none of the characters look at it, the chair is the emotional and visual core of the shot, its frame blacker than any shadow, the arms and seat polished to become eerily luminous.

EDWARD G. ROBINSON IS ON THE OTHER SIDE OF THE DARK MIRROR as Keyes in *Double Indemnity*. In this scene cut from the final release of the film, Walter Neff (Fred MacMurray) awaits execution, the "end of the line" of the criminal journey on which he embarked with femme fatale Phyllis Dietrichson. Here the drab gray comes from the exterior walls of the execution chamber, as the overhead light on Neff turns his eyes into black pools and models the cheek, so in his last moments his visage becomes a skull-like death mask. The foreground rail which Keyes clutches creates a darker gray line of separation. The bolts around the air-tight window through which Neff is visible are the grotesque ornamentation of a noir frame. For Keyes, anguished over his protege's fate, this frame is both a picture and a mirror of that anguish.

MOTIF

Face and Gesture

OPPOSED TO THE EXTERNALIZATION OF NATURALISM AND Impressionism, painterly Expressionism relies on stylization to reveal man's inner state, a state often marked by anxiety or worse. This tendency goes back at least to Edvard Munch and is well represented here in Erich Heckel's *Portrait of a Man* (figure 1, 1919), a woodcut in which the pale green of the face and hands plays off against a background of blue and brown. These unusual colors, together with the black, angular lines of the block print, suggest an apprehension bordering on neurosis. The nearest equivalent to such mannerism in the German cinema was the stylized performances of certain of its actors who were informed by an expressionist school of acting whose source was the theater of Max Reinhardt. Among the most adept at this rhetorical, exaggerated style of acting was Conrad Veidt, here in *The Hands of Orlac* (figure 2, 1924) performing a gesture quite representative of this school. Such expressionistic acting was not very compatible with the American naturalistic style, so film noir was forced to rely on conventions of lighting and Hollywood's skill at typage (essentially type-casting to face and feature), making use of more subtle gestures to suggest inner states. The success of film noir in achieving this can be measured in the two final illustrations: actor Jack Lambert's features (figure 3, *The Killers*—1946) and Richard Widmark's expression (figure 4, *Night and the City*—1950).   —ROBERT PORFIRIO

Figure 1

Figure 2

Figure 3

Figure 4

MOTIF

Dream and Flashback

THOUGH IT PREDATES THE CLASSIC PERIOD OF FILM NOIR, Blind Alley (1939) is an unusual gangster film for the thirties because of its heavy psychological orientation. The film, which tells how the homicidal proclivities of its protagonist, Hal Wilson (Chester Morris), are exorcised through the efforts of a psychiatrist (Ralph Bellamy), is based on a successful play by James Warwick. The film, however, draws on the talents of its émigré director Charles Vidor and its fledgling cinematographer Lucien Ballard to represent Wilson's inner states in a highly expressionistic manner. A recurrent nightmare that is linked to Wilson's hydrophobia—he is locked in a cage during a rainstorm with only an umbrella for protection—is rendered in negative (figure 1), creating a rare, startling effect but one that had been used years before in the German expressionist classic Nosferatu. Once the psychiatrist interprets the dream, Wilson is able to recall the childhood trauma that is the source of his problems. The flashback which details the trauma forsakes the optical trickery of the dream sequence, resorting instead to sets whose distortions and angularities are classically expressionistic (figure 2). This flashback also involves an early use of aural expressionism, eliminating all naturalistic sounds in favor of a silence which is only broken by Wilson's voice-over narration.

Recognized by many as the first true film noir, Stranger on the Third Floor (1940) overcomes the weaknesses of a very modest budget with a visual bravura that would become part of the RKO noir style, perhaps because of the early combination of cinematographer Nicholas Musuraca and art director Albert D'Agostino. The

Figure 1

high point of its visual expressionism is a long dream sequence during which the hero's nightmare—he is arrested, tried, and executed for a murder he did not commit—is presented in a strongly expressionist montage sequence (figures 3-7) featuring John McGuire in the lead. The effect of the sequence is heightened by oblique camera angles, unusual graphic design, and actors whose stylized gestures (e.g., figures 3 and 6) are reminiscent of an earlier Germanic school.

—ROBERT PORFIRIO

Figure 2

Figure 3

Figure 4

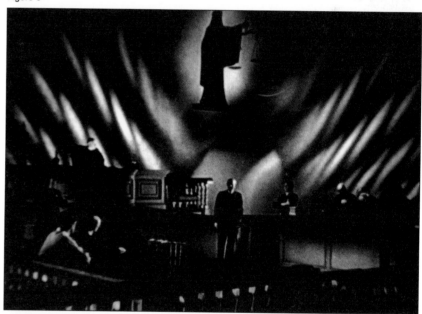

Figure 5

Figure 6

Figure 7

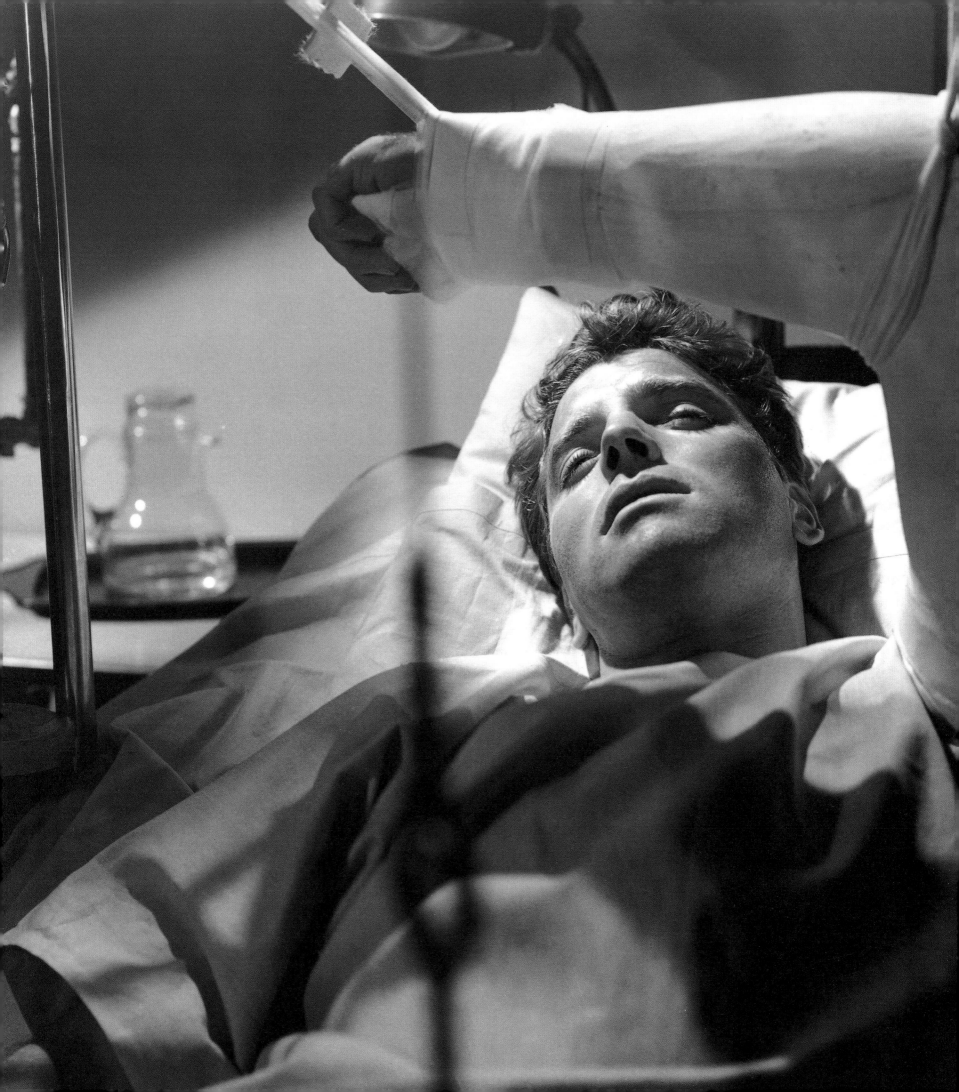

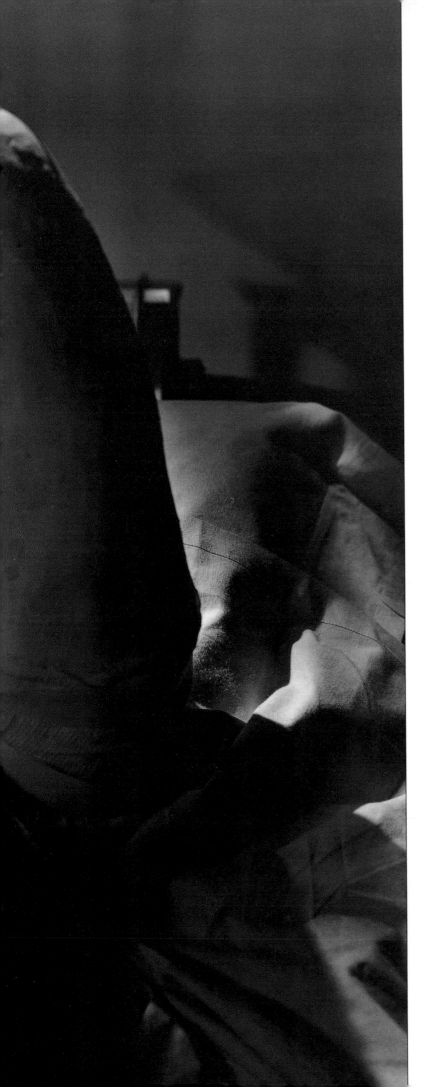

CHAPTER FIVE

THE RECKLESS MOMENT

As Al Roberts says in his oft-quoted remark from *Detour* "someday fate or some mysterious force can put the finger on you or me for no reason at all." The film noir protagonists who are afflicted by this mysterious force are a diverse group. Whether obsessive or avaricious, alienated or incarcerated, backed up into a dark corner or staring into a dark mirror, there is often a defining moment when fate points the finger for these characters. *Amour fou* or mad love combines many of these emotions and can lead to a conscious recklessness, as with Steve Thompson's lament of his loss of control in *Criss Cross*: "From the start it all went one way. It was in the cards or it was fate...or whatever you want to call it."

STEVE THOMPSON (BURT LANCASTER) LIES IN THE HOSPITAL AFTER DOUBLE-crossing his co-conspirators in CRISS CROSS (1949), a title that instantly evokes the treacherous traps in which noir protagonists find themselves. It is Thompson's obsessive involvement with his ex-wife Anna which leads him into a criminal act and eventually this entrapped posture. His arm in a cast dominates the foreground, a tangible symbol of his suffering, while his semi-conscious expression is modeled by an unseen source light above and behind him. While his face lying on the white pillow is the visual core of the shot, the array of bars, pulleys, counterweights, slings, and shadows which surround him create the figurative reality for Thompson, helplessly entrapped by his own recklessness and obsession. The fact that his own arm closes the trap, surrounds and pins him down in the two dimensions of the shot, confirms that he has brought this on himself.

I N HIS EARLIER NOIR FILM, *CAUGHT* (1949), MAX OPHULS USED THE DARK corners of Ohlrig's mansion to externalize the disturbed mental state of its owner. The household of Lucia Harper (Joan Bennett) is a full-lit, everyday, upper middle-class setting, revealing some worn, commonplace surfaces, into which little thought of criminal acts, cover-ups, and blackmail was likely to enter. But in the context of film noir this is precisely what can happen. As she watches two petty criminals Nagle (Roy Roberts) and Donnelly (James Mason) struggle over her, Lucia's emotional position is visually encapsulated. In contrast to earlier more glamorous portrayals, such as the mysterious Alice in *Woman in the Window* or even the newlywed Celia in *Secret Beyond the Door*, Bennett is made to look older and more matronly. Her gray dress is tailored, even elegant, and her short hair is styled; but both are far removed from the dark allure of the woman in the window. In this neutral color, she blends with the decor, while Nagle and Donnelly, who wants to protect Lucia for his former accomplice, stand out in their dark suit and coat. They intrude visually and their criminality intrudes into Lucia's ordered world, and she cringes before both these intrusions, emotional and physical, at once.

F RITZ LANG'S *THE WOMAN IN THE WINDOW* IS A MORE TYPICAL DEFINITION OF a reckless moment in film noir. Richard Wanley (Edward G. Robinson, kneeling) holds the weapon he has used to kill Alice Reed's (Joan Bennett) boyfriend Mazard (Arthur Loft, prone on the floor). His chance encounter with this beautiful femme fatale outside a window displaying her portrait has led him to her deco apartment and the crime which will be his undoing. Dressed in black to set off her white skin, Alice's classic beauty is visually connected to the small female form on the mantel. Her image reflected in the mirror in the background, both hints at her duplicitous character and links her to the sculpture which underlines her erotic power. Wanley is clearly subservient in the frame. He kneels before her, offering up the weapon to her. His image is also reflected in the backgrond, foreshadowing the double life he will have to live in order to escape apprehension by the police.

THE JOHN ALTON-PHOTOGRAPHED FILM *RAW DEAL* (1948) ENCAPSULATES THE love triangle so common to film noir in this single shot. In the foreground, Joe Sullivan (Dennis O'Keefe) and Ann Martin (Marsha Hunt) form an embrace. They stare lovingly into each other's eyes. Ann, in her moment of recklessness, has given herself over to a man who proves to be a violent felon and eventually drags her into his world of crime. But while a distorted shadow falls on her face, there is nothing overtly sinister in this pose, in which the gray tones of clothing and hair are matched. In the background to the right stands Pat (Claire Trevor), Joe's former girl. Her face reveals a slight shock but is also resolute, which is reinforced by her position with a right arm thrust out on the banister, in affirmation of strength rather than supporting herself. Her sizing, clothing, and the rim light on her hair further distinguish her from Joe and Ann. Even more notable is the use of the bars and banisters to indicate the tug of emotions between Pat and the two lovers. The diagonals form a point at right, the direction towards which Ann leans back slightly. Neither the couple nor Pat are at the vector point. Rather they are on different tracks heading for an emotional collision there. There are no less than four sets of bars in the shot, including the shadow in the background. These criss-crossing bars not only signify separation but also symbolize the web of betrayal inappropriate love has woven around the three characters.

IN ANOTHER TRIANGULAR COMPOSITION FROM *THE POSTMAN ALWAYS RINGS Twice* the three-way dynamic has been reconfigured. Cora (Lana Turner) and Frank Chambers (John Garfield, left) have killed Cora's husband and disassembled the earlier, more traditional triangle. Now the triangle is a legal one and the conflict is between the individual's instinct for self-preservation and love for the other. The sexual component which motivated their crime is removed with their incarceration and their enmeshment by the legal system, evident in the criss-crossing shadows on the walls behind them and the real bars on the right side of the frame. The portly legal assistant in the foreground (Alan Reed) offers a pen to Cora which she can use to make a deal and save herself. Her upright figure dressed in white at frame center is also the apex of the triangle. As she looks down apprehensively at the pen, the wheel-chair ridden Chambers sits resignedly behind her, legs draped so that he mirrors the lawyer at the desk, completing the triangle. The tense geometry of the shot is fleeting and will be ruptured whether Cora bends to sign or turns back towards Chambers.

MARION CRANE (JANET LEIGH) IN ALFRED HITCHCOCK'S LATE NOIR *Psycho* (1960) is a character who is trapped by a reckless moment rooted in her dissatisfaction with her life and ambivalent love (Sam Loomis, played by John Gavin). In order to improve their lives she steals. The bars on her and her lover's face as the sun streams in through the wooden shutters foreshadows the crime she will commit as well as the punishment both fate and Norman Bates will inflict on her. The bars also externalize the trap that fate is setting for her as she contemplates her "way out" of her more mundane financial constrictions. Her dominance in the affair is indicated by Sam's seemingly disembodied head which rests on her left shoulder while her left hand seems to press his head to hers in a gentle, yet forceful gesture. Hitchcock's world view always postulates a chaotic undercurrent running through the ordered world and his evocation of the everyday to create irony is typical of late classic period noir, where Marion's reckless impulse can lead to the wildly disturbed events at Bates Motel.

AS IN THE IMAGES FROM *SUDDEN FEAR* AND *DUEL IN THE SUN*, MICHAEL O'Hara (Orson Welles) dominates this frame from *The Lady from Shanghai* (1948). In fact, the black hat and coat block the frame even more completely than in previous examples. Elsa Bannister (Rita Hayworth) is totally hemmed in by the dark mass of O'Hara's body and the door at left. With a soft overhead light falling on her she seems small, demure, even fragile, her white-gloved hands clasped lightly as if appealing for help. She looks up imploringly to the black hulk looming over her. Unlike the female figures in *Sudden Fear* or *Duel in the Sun*, there is neither fear nor defiance in Elsa's look. She is the visual center and her look gives her control. For as she implores O'Hara with her eyes, she creates the mischance which will drag him down, a willing victim seduced by her charms into her corrupt world. What the spectator sees here and in other scenes in the movie is a subtle subjectification, Elsa seen from the perspective of O'Hara who loves and wants to believe her.

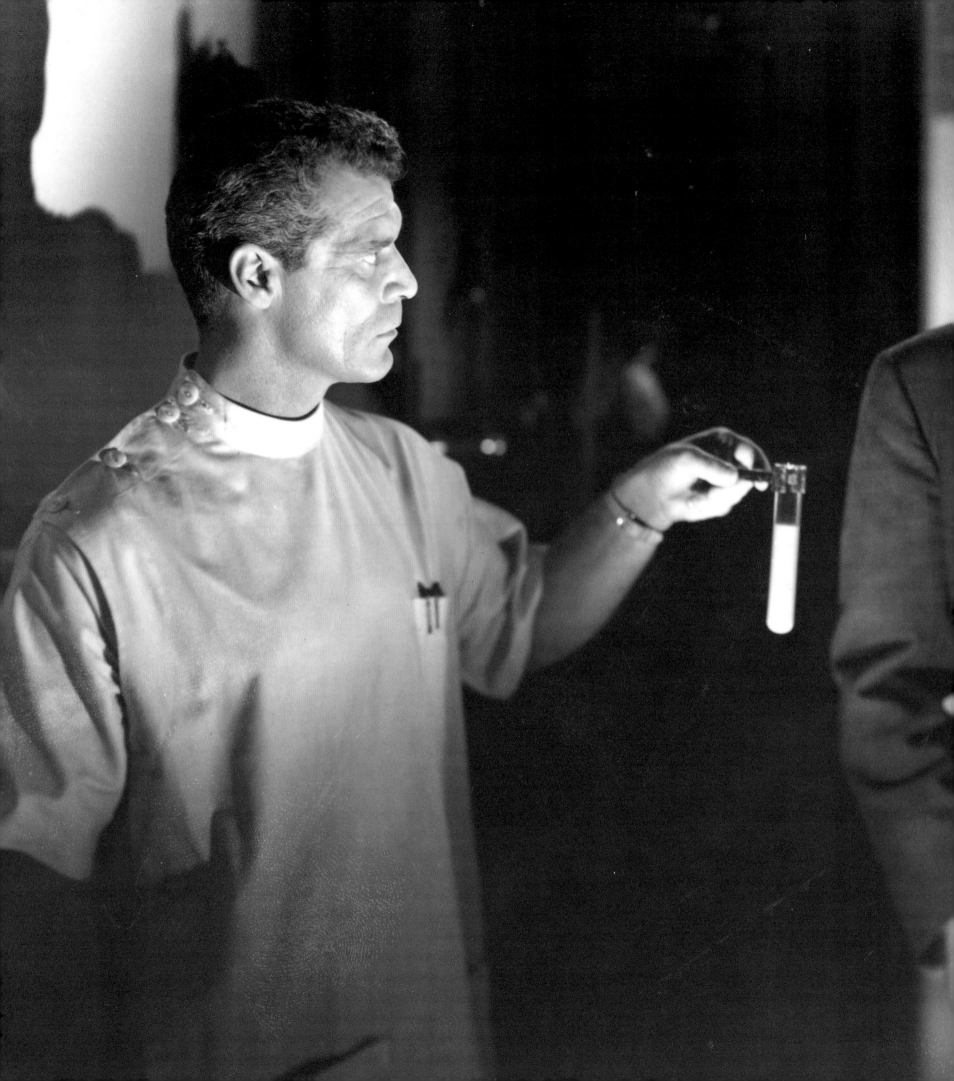

I N THE MOST IRONIC OF FILM NOIR, THESE RECKLESS MOMENTS can be absurdly arbitrary. The plot of *DOA* (1950) centers on Frank Bigelow (Edmond O'Brien, right) who is here informed by a doctor (Frank Gerstle) that he has a fatal iridium poisoning. The rest of the film is his patently existential search to find the reason why. The absurd, as Camus personified it, slaps Bigelow in the face when he discovers that he was poisoned not by any personal enemy but through complete mischance. His "reckless" moment was simply being in the wrong place at the wrong time, a fatal inattention and true existential nightmare. In both body language and expression, as he learns that he is doomed, Bigelow vividly demonstrates his shock. He seems frozen in motion: his head snapped towards the bearer of bad news, his eyes bulging, his tie swinging loose from his jacket, his hands stiff at his side. His head and body seem almost to be moving in opposite directions. At center frame is, of course, the culprit, the glowing vial of iridium. It draws attention by its position and by its eerie whiteness contrasting vividly with the dark background and so powerful that it illuminates both faces from below and casts a shadow on the left wall. The doctor contrasts with Bigelow's frenzy by his calm but serious expression and his steady gesture of extending the vial towards Bigelow as if offering him a closer look at the murderous chemical that is already eating away at his system, a calmness and steadiness which Bigelow realizes he will never have again.

FRAMED (1947) IS TYPICAL OF FILM NOIR'S REVEALING TITLES. The situation of Mike Lambert (Glenn Ford, right) is tied to another femme fatale; but Lambert is no patsy; and, in fact, his would-be exploiter ultimately falls for him. His pose, setting, and expression is that of a classic noir protagonist. He leans on the counter of the bar for support, as he distractedly holds a cigarette. His hat is cocked to one side as if reflecting his uncertainty, reinforced by the sympathetic look of the bartender (Sid Tomack) over Lambert's shoulder. The glistening fixtures of the bar set off Lambert's solid gray figure as a high placed key light to his right front softly models his features. Everything in the shot tells the viewer that Lambert is poised on the brink of something, which in the context of film noir is likely and turns out to be his own reckless moment.

ALEX WINKLEY (BILL WILLIAMS, RIGHT) SUCCUMBS TO THE TEMPTATION OF A one-night stand and is marked as a killer in the adaptation of Cornell Woolrich's *Deadline at Dawn* (1946). Enlisting the aid of Gus (Paul Lukas) and June (Susan Hayward), he follows every exculpatory lead in a race against the clock typical of Woolrich's work. The low angle, tilted off horizontal, used in this shot is a visual motif often associated with imbalance in film noir. In this shot, it distorts the size of the shadows behind the characters. As June looks fearfully towards Gus and grabs at his shirt, both men stare at something on the floor. While their uniforms and badges (Gus is cab driver and the badge his hack number; Winkley's chevrons are turned towards camera) should symbolize social order, they offer no consolation. It doesn't take much for the viewer to guess why that is. With the characters looming over the spectator, the angle and low light transform an ordinary room into an ominous setting.

IN ANOTHER WOOLRICH TWIST OF FATE, HELEN FERGUSON (BARBARA Stanwyck) in *No Man of Her Own* (1950) survives a train crash and recklessly decides to take the identity of a dead woman in order to escape her past. In this composition Helen searches for security in the arms of her new love Bill Harkness (John Lund). Harkness dominates the frame with his height, the bulk of his light gray coat, and the comforting clasp of his left hand on Helen's arm. He also radiates security by his mature looks and serious yet assured gaze over his shoulder. Helen, on the other hand, reflects insecurity. Her face, tilted upward towards Bill, is pleading. Her body is indistinct in her black coat, neither arms nor hands visible. It seems as if, rather than being hemmed in, she blocks the door in order to be swallowed up by him in the two dimensions of the frame and to escape detection.

HOWARD TYLER (FRANK LOVEJOY, LEFT) IN *TRY AND GET ME* (1950) IS AS MUCH A VICTIM of the social system around him as of his own recklessness. In order to feed his family, he commits the crime for which he is incarcerated. More typically scenes of protagonists behind bars use bars to isolate them or separate them from loved ones. In this shot, at right of the frame is Sheriff Demig (Cliff Clark), who regards Tyler with compassionate detachment. The slight angle reveals the width of the cross bars as they cut through Tyler's face and torso. The foreshortened bunk behind seems to press against him, so that he has almost no room. The irony, for the contrite, non-menacing Tyler, head bowed, hands in full view, is that the bars are actually his protection from an angry lynch mob. Although the sheriff is outside the bars and Howard inside, they are both subjects of the legal system which the bars symbolize.

O FTEN EXCORIATED BY CONTEMPORARY CRITICS FOR THE VIOLENCE OF PICTURES LIKE *TRY AND Get Me* (also known as *The Sound of Fury*), film noir did often depict harsh and deadly behaviors in an everyday manner. A reckless moment and a murder accusation have already landed seaman Bill Saunders (Burt Lancaster) in *Kiss the Blood of My Hands* (1948) in jail where he is subjected to a caning that resembles a medieval-style torture. At center frame Saunders is trussed up like a Christ figure between two symmetrical beams to which is his body is lashed. His face still registers defiance as he looks back to the shadows at the guard who is about to strike him. He is the emotional as well as dynamic center of this composition, heightened by the key light on him and the scaffolding and by his pseudo-crucified like pose. In addition, the two guards, one in the foreground securing Joe with a rope and one in the background with the cane, create an action diagonal in the frame centered again on Saunders.

JOHNNY MCQUEEN (JAMES MASON) IN CAROL REED'S *Odd Man Out* (1947) is a wounded Irish revolutionary attempting to flee the country after a bombing. His devotion to the cause and his status as a suffering victim, gradually dying from a gunshot wound, establish his martyr-complex. His position against the railings on the left of the frame with his right arm extended upward visually creates a crucifixion motif that is partly subjective and partly objective. He looks at the center of the frame towards a short tunnel and an open square, which alternately represent freedom or death. The clock tower is an emphatic reminder that hunted and wounded, little time remains for him. Both sides of the iron fence reach to the opposite edges of the frame forming a forced perspective and cutting out other routes for McQueen. As his lover Kathleen (Kathleen Ryan) walks towards him from the background through the passage, the snow which covers the ground and clings to his coat and hair is emblematic of the purity which he has lost. These divided perceptions are carried over into Kathleen's face, deeply side-lit in a traditional invocation of indecision. As back light strikes her shoulder and glints off her hair to form a halo, Kathleen has an angelic quality as she approaches, his last hope for freedom or redemption before dying.

WHILE IT HARDLY SEEMED RECKLESS, GUY HAINES'S (FARLEY Granger, right) chance encounter has unwittingly involved him in an exchange of murders with Bruno Antony (Robert Walker) in another shot from Hitchcock's *Strangers on a Train* (1951). While they may not be as alike as Antony has claimed, the two characters are in many ways emotional doppelgangers, underlined by this shot. From a high angle and more distant perspective with rim light catching their dark, wavy hair, the similarity of their physical features is emphasized. As they stand at opposite ends of the frame facing each other, they are both in three-quarter profile to the spectator, creating a further balance in the frame. Subtle differences give Anthony dominance: he is carrying a gun in his right hand; he commands the attention of both Guy and the mastiff; and he is framed by two candlesticks in the background. But, Anthony points the Luger at the floor and is also blocked by a railing in the foreground, indicating that he is more of a trapped figure psychologically than Haines, whose full figure is visible and seems to have an open path away from Haines.

IMMATURITY CAUSES GEORGE LA MAIN (JOHN BARRYMORE, JR., LEFT) IN *The Big Night* (1951) to spend his own reckless night culminating in a charge of attempted murder. His mental tension is externalized in this composition as George confronts the man who beat his father, Al Judge (Howard St. John). George's expression is one of hatred and confusion, as he clutches a gun in his right hand. The gun is again an unscarred icon, as George's finger is well off the trigger with his hand wrapped completely around it. Al Judge returns his look, with his own right hand grasping a cane. The small desk lamp between them is tilted also adding to the instability as it throws a maze of shadows on the walls. Both characters are poised as if they are about to pounce. Although Judge is sitting while George stands, he is not dominated by the boy. His fierce looks, his dark suit, and the menace of his slightly upraised cane make him a formidable adversary.

IN ANOTHER ENGLISH NOIR, *THE THIRD MAN* (1949) DIRECTED BY CAROL Reed, Harry Lime (Orson Welles) cringes behind access stairs in the sewers of Vienna. In the desperate moral milieu of postwar Vienna as scripted by novelist Graham Greene, Lime's cynical self-assurance must inevitably lead to his entrapment. This single close shot encapsulates his fate. Cornered, the massive iron steps hinder rather than protect, as the supports, handrail, and mass of bricks turn the sewer into a prison. Lime's small caliber handgun is dwarfed by the structure, his face is cut top and bottom and his brow shadowed by it, revealing only his desperate expression, wide-eyed with fear. The fingers of his other hand, begrimed by the chase, grip the step in a futile and awkward gesture.

THE GUN IS ALMOST NEVER OUT OF HIRED KILLER PHILLIP RAVEN'S (ALAN Ladd) hand in *This Gun for Hire*, adapted from a Graham Greene novel. Unlike Lime, Raven is not cornered by his own carelessness. Rather he is set up by the man who contracts for his services. Raven has his own strict code, in which betrayal is a much more grievous offense than murder. Even though he disapproves of her vulgar behavior, as he menaces Annie (Pamela Blake) within the dark confines of a telephone booth, Raven has no real intention of shooting her. Not only would that reveal his presence to the nearby authorities but it would be inappropriate. Although the edges of his face are shadowed by his hat and other objects, a square of light falls over his features, as he regards Annie with complete detachment. Raven's finger is on the trigger and a highlight along the gun barrel forms a vector pointing right at her throat. But Raven's eyes glance at her face without malice. For Raven violence and even murder are casual acts, as the style of the shot confirms.

THE DOOR IN *HE RAN ALL THE WAY* (1951) ACTS AS A BARRIER THAT IS both physical and psychological between Nick Robey (John Garfield) and Peg Dobbs (Shelley Winters). While Peg loves the fugitive Robey, her family—her father (Wallace Ford) and little brother (Bobby Hyatt)—represent the normal life she may lose by clinging to Nick. Nick's distraught expression and forceful grip on his gun, which in the two dimensions of the frame points right at the child, underscores the volatile nature which has made him a fugitive. His look is apprehensive but determined as he presses against his own shadow on the back of the door. Peg's expression is more conflicted, mouth open, eyes unfocused, hand on the edge of the door, as her loyalties are divided between Nick and her family. She is physically divided from them by the door which splits the frame vertically, and she is on the same side of it as Nick. Mr. Dobbs and Peg's brother, who looks up imploring past the door chain that cuts across his head, occupy a much smaller portion of the frame in relation to Peg and Nick, indicating their lack of power in the scene.

I N FRITZ LANG'S *HUMAN DESIRE* (1954) JEFF WARREN (GLENN FORD, left) and Vicki Buckley (Gloria Grahame) are adulterous lovers meeting in secret who hide as a train watchman checks the yard. They cringe in the shadows behind the door while the watchman and his flaring light dominate the center frame, forcing the spectator to concentrate on his presence. Whether or not the viewer sees the light as a symbol of the examining eye of society, which is bent on thwarting their love, Lang's particular determinism informs the noir style over and over again, spanning two decades from *You Only Live Once* through *Woman in the Window* to *Beyond a Reasonable Doubt*, as he visually records the consequences of reckless and unsanctioned behavior. Although Vicki is behind Jeff, her face cut off by his collar, she seems to merge with and support him, while he draws back apprehensively. So completely are they joined in two dimensions that the gray folds in her skirt and his pants leg seem part of the same fabric. The dinginess of the line shack underscores the sordidness of their affair, as the streaked panes of the window behind the lovers reinforces the squalid mood. The door with its cross-hatched shadows is also an important icon, a dual emblem of entrapment and evasion, the dual emotions with which all Lang's noir characters must grapple.

THE DOOR IN THIS WELL-KNOWN IMAGE FROM *DOUBLE INDEMNITY* ACTS AS A LITERAL AND figurative barrier. It shields Phyllis Dietrichson (Barbara Stanwyck) from the prying eyes of Keyes, the insurance investigator who has come to see agent Walter Neff (Fred MacMurray) and is off frame where Neff apprehensively directs his gaze. While she hides behind it, seeming much smaller in the frame in relation to the anxious Neff, her expression is nonetheless impassive. Place and Peterson remark that the "undiffused lighting of Barbara Stanwyck . . . creates a hard-edged, mask-like surface beauty. By comparison 'hard-boiled' Fred MacMurray seems soft and vulnerable." Exactly how "hard-boiled" MacMurray's persona may be is open to question, but the flat lighting does distinguish Phyllis's smooth features from the modeling on Neff's. Still in two dimensions there is a strange visual conjunction between them, even as the door separates them, for Neff's shadow on the door blends in with Phyllis's figure so that it almost seems like he is joined to her left shoulder. The door may symbolize the barrier of mistrust between these two lovers and conspirators while Phyllis, the temptress in the recess behind Neff, may also personify the criminal lurking in his id. It is clear that, although smaller, Phyllis has dominance in this reckless relationship.

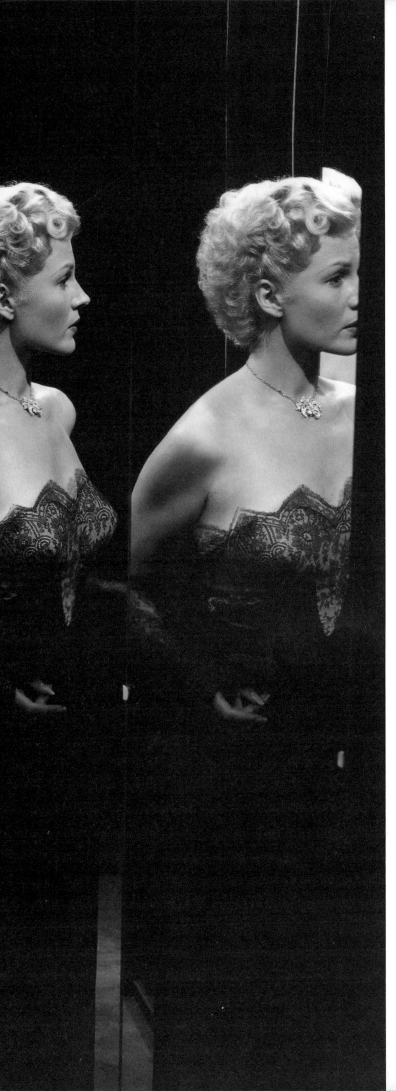

CHAPTER SIX

NIGHT HAS A THOUSAND EYES

In discussing anti-traditional staging, Place and Peterson remark that "mirror reflections, beyond their symbolic representations of fragmented ego or idealized image, sometimes assume ominous and foreboding qualities solely because they are so compositionally prominent. It is common for a character to form constant balanced two-shots of himself and his own mirror reflection or shadow. Such compositions, though superficially balanced, begin to lose their stability in the course of the film as the symbolic Doppelganger either is shown to lack its apparent substantiality or else proves to be a dominant and destructive alter ego."

THE FEMME FATALE IS DOUBLED AND REDOUBLED IN THE FINAL SEQUENCE OF *THE LADY FROM Shanghai* (1948) and radically changed in the process. The real Elsa Bannister (Rita Hayworth) is at the left edge of the shot. In an angle taken from the protagonist's point of view, she looks directly at the camera, and yet her attitude is hard to read. The intricate pattern of her gown carried over to her semi-gloved hands which she holds at her side creates a visual confusion. Her expression is open, perhaps apprehensive, perhaps questioning, as a high, undiffused key light sharply models her brow and her sculpted hair, so that she almost resembles a statue. The reflection directly behind her reveals the set of her shoulders, emphasizing the rigidity of her figure. The viewer knows that the "real" Elsa has conspired in crime and betrayed her lover. Yet the panel of mirrors to the right, where she seems to slowly turn her head, the same hand and the expression now seem to telegraph an appeal for help. The same bare shoulders that were strong are now vulnerable. The darker curls behind her head are softer. Even the expression, seen in profile in the last two panels, seems more to plead for help. As the fun house mirrors shatter the frame and reveal the many faces of the femme fatale, the spectator participates with the protagonist in seeing all these aspects, so that the shot renders both a literal (or physical) point of view and a figurative (or emotional) one as well.

EDWARD G. ROBINSON'S PORTRAYAL OF THE DOOMED PSYCHIC TRITON IN *NIGHT HAS A THOUSAND EYES* (1948) is a 180 degree turn from Rico in *Little Caesar* or Canelli in *Black Tuesday*. The conceit of the title is typical of novelist Cornell Woolrich. While Dashiell Hammett and Raymond Chandler are commonly regarded as the preeminent literary sources of a noir style, and writers such as Steve Fisher, Horace McCoy, Jim Thompson, and W.R. Burnett form a second tier, no writer's work was adapted into film noir as often as that of Woolrich. But Woolrich's off-beat tales were not proto-typically noir. He disdained much of the "tough guy" posturing of the hard-boiled noir tradition and, in fact, often reversed the gender roles of the period. Woolrich also indulged in temporal and spatial distortions that deviated widely from the fundamentally realist style of crime fiction and film noir. It was Woolrich's male and female heroes with their obsessive and alienated outlooks which were a perfect fit for film noir's classic period.

For a viewer whose genre expectations of E.G. Robinson are as a "hard case," the character's fear and confusion play against type. As he stands before the mirror Triton looks at his hand for traces of the blood which he has "seen" on his shirt. In this shot, it is the mirror image which is in focus. Although that image is clearly confined within a carved frame, the sharpness gives it preeminence over its material counterpart, the actual Triton. Just as the imaginary blood will become real, the mirror world of visions is already real for Triton. In the two dimensions of the frame, the two figures have different stature. The "real" Triton in the foreground is larger but stands in silhouette. The mirror Triton is smaller but his whole puzzled expression is visible to the viewer. At frame center, the hands of the figures intersect. Triton abandons everyone he knows because he cannot cope with his visions of when and how people will die, cannot imagine seeing the death of loved ones. From Triton's distorted perspective, the starry sky contains a thousand eyes that peer down relentlessly at him.

THE STYLISTIC OVERLAY IN THE TWO SHOT OF MARTIN ROME (RICHARD Conte) and Lt. Candella (Victor Mature) in *Cry of the City* (1948) also relies on typing and doubling. The two men, who come from the same immigrant neighborhood, are now on opposite sides of the law. Their figures are roughly the same size as they face each other at opposite sides of the frame. Yet as Candella questions Rome, the white hospital gown and diffused key light that rims his hair and masks his jaw line, give Rome a softer aspect. As he reclines, only the clenched hands on the bed covers suggest Rome's criminal determination. Candela's dark suit separates him graphically from all the other elements in the room, where even the chairs and bedposts are white, and drains his body of natural contour, leaving a wedge-shaped mass from which his head and hand protrude awkwardly. The light which strikes Candela full face as he leans forward gives him a drawn look. At the center of the frame the other dark object, handcuffs attached to the bed frame, hang ominously. Since the viewer clearly knows which character is heroic and which is villainous, posture and costume play against type and add visual tension.

I N THE KENDO SEQUENCE FROM *CRIMSON KIMONO* (1959) TWO policemen who are longtime friends and partners, Kojaku (James Shigeta) and Bancroft (Glenn Corbett), square off in a mock duel. Both men love the same woman, but Kojaku is angry by what he believes is Bancroft's racist reaction. In the kimonos and face masks, the two men are indistinguishable. When the combat turns vicious, the viewer cannot tell which of the men has lost control. The doppelganger effect forces the audience to confront its own prejudices about stereotypes and behavior.

IN *NOTORIOUS* (1946) ALICIA HUBERMAN (INGRID BERGMAN, CENTER) has married Alexander Sebastian (Claude Rains) to prove her loyalty and help unmask him as a Nazi. Sebastian and his mother (Madame Constantin, left) have discovered Huberman's duplicity and are slowly poisoning her. The two Sebastians, mother and son, mirror each other as they lean forward in profile. Reacting to these doubles, Alicia looks perplexed. Their matching poses in the foreground, from the arch of their backs to the tilt of their noses, hem Alicia in almost completely, as the line of the bed frame above them completes the two-dimensional enclosure symbolic of her entrapment.

THE SYMBOLIC VALUES IN THIS SHOT OF JOAN CRAWFORD AS THE TITLE character in *Mildred Pierce* (1945) are equally overt. Crawford's square jaw along with the padded shoulders and bulk of her fur coat emphasize her mannish aspect, Unable to come to terms with the betrayal by those she loves, her vacant stare and parted lips, as well the shadow which cuts her face diagonally into light and dark halves, all reflect her indecision. The bust of Beethoven to her left is literally just a piece of set decoration. "Often," Place and Peterson notes, "objects in the frame take on an assumed importance simply because they act to determine a stable composition." Here the object does more than balance the frame. Its placement higher in the frame and the highlights that glint off the dark surface draw the viewer's attention away from Mildred. The bust's hair and nose mirror Mildred's, who is, like the sculpture, figuratively frozen and emotionally "disarmed" by the events of the narrative.

EVEN WITHOUT POINT OF VIEW, THE NOIR MIRROR CAN CREATE AN EMOTIONAL DOPPELGANGER which personifies the literal character's mental state. The self-absorbed Waldo Lydecker (Clifton Webb) in *Laura* cannot help but smile when he peers at himself in a reflecting glass. In the mirror, he is the übermensch he believes himself to be. The viewer can objectively see the ungainly way in which Lydecker's suspenders hold up his pants, the unattractive folds in the back of his shirt, and the array of brushes and lotions on the dresser top. In the mirror, Lydecker is smooth and unblemished. In the mirror, even Detective McPherson (Dana Andrews) who has come to question Lydecker about a murder, appears to be a supplicant, holding an offering in his hands and head bowed as he glances up at the superior being. The figure within the frame is merely Lydecker's reflection, but the world in the mirror is his world, arrayed according to monomania.

N NARRATIVE TERMS, LT. CORNELL (RICHARD BOONE) IN VICKI (1953) IS CLOSER TO MCPHERSON THAN TO
Lydecker. In psychological terms the reverse is true. In the earlier illustrations from the two films,
the decor and the staging suggested that Cornell's obsession with a female victim was more
profound and disturbed than McPherson's. The mirror shot of Cornell by the cigarette machine
actually contains both of the doppelgangers which Place and Peterson cite: a shadow behind
him and a mirror image in front. The key light up and to the right causes the shadow to stretch across
the rear wall. The lack of fill light on Cornell's back causes the shadow to merge with his figure. This
could be read as a darker half, the part of Cornell's psyche which has fixated on Vicki and taken
his being over emotionally. Alternately the long slope of the shoulder and the symmetry of the hat
brim could represent the solid, by-the-book cop which Cornell once was. As Cornell turns to light a
cigarette, he glances back possibly towards someone off-screen or possibly towards his own shadow.
The mirror image is also unsettling. It is a blurry profile over which dark lettering is superimposed. The
decorative pattern etched in the surface distort the line of Cornell's hands and make them appear
crippled or claw-like. Between the two figures, light reflected from the mirror forms a wedge on the
dingy wall. Compared to the solid, efficient bulk of the machine itself, an emblem of social order,
this broken form literally reflects off Cornell and is an emblem of his disturbance.

THERE ARE ALSO TWO DOUBLES IN THIS SHOT FROM *New York Confidential* (1955). Nick Magellan (Richard Conte) has followed orders and killed his friend, quisling mob boss Charlie Lupo (Broderick Crawford). Magellan's expression reveals his distaste for the task but also his stoic resolve while regarding the body of his victim in the foreground. Counterposed with his shadow on the rear wall is a cylindrical form. Unlike Cornell's, Magellan's shadow is separated from his form by fill light which lightens the shadow and backlight on Magellan. Despite the thin shadow, Magellan's trenchcoated form is arrayed against a dingy wall like a dense, black cut-out. That form does blend with another double, the body of Lupo, their legs merging so that the recumbent Lupo stretches out before Magellan like a second shadow. As Magellan himself will shortly be killed, an event which the spectator probably expects, this second double is equally if not more portentous than the first.

THE FRAGMENTS OF THE MIRROR

ALFRED HITCHCOCK'S RELATIONSHIP TO THE NOIR STYLE IS even more difficult to define than Woolrich's. *Shadow of a Doubt, Notorious, Strangers on a Train*, even *The Wrong Man*, a title which could describe a whole sub-set of noir films, all have elements which qualify them as noir but none are core examples of the noir movement. In terms of narrative, *The Paradine Case, Psycho*, even *Stage Fright* could be noir; but are they? Doubles and mirror images are stylistic keys to *Vertigo* (1958). The obsessed detective hero even refers to the dreams of his client's wife as "fragments of a mirror." Yet *Vertigo* is so reliant on the point of view of this character for its dramatic impact, that it lacks a sense of a noir underworld, of an undercurrent of fatality and menace that, as Al Roberts noted, "can put the finger on you or me for no reason at all." In the process of transforming Judy (Kim Novak) into his lost love Madeleine, Scottie Ferguson (James Stewart) must bring her into his perception of reality. In this mirror shot, he looks at and through Judy trying to see the woman he wants within. The mirrored panels behind her do not reveal an alternate or more appealing perspective. It is because he is cognizant of the dichotomy between real and imagined that Ferguson is troubled. The image he seeks is beyond both the literal woman proximate to him and her reflection beyond. There is no added stylistic comment from lighting, angle, etc. because Ferguson's point of view is the overriding factor.

N *THE BIG COMBO* (1955), DETECTIVE DIAMOND (CORNEL WILDE) speaks with his sometime girlfriend Rita (Helene Stanton). She knows he has taken advantage of her and is angry. The faded flowers, little Buddha and doll's head on her dressing table, suggest a real person in contrast with the array in front of Waldo Lydecker's mirror. Since Diamond loves another woman (and Rita knows it), his feelings for Rita are far from obsessive. While Rita may be an exotic dancer, the other woman is a gangster's moll; yet Diamond has less respect for Rita. Even in her flimsy costume, he regards her with little carnal interest. As he leans in, blocking her light and encroaching on her reflection on the center panel, she uses a hand mirror to avoid seeing him. Still it is clear from her expression that she is emotionally engaged and susceptible to his entreaties. As she sits sideways on a stool, the source light cuts across her arms and torso making her look exposed and vulnerable. The same light makes Diamond, who has not bothered to remove his hat, seem stiff and severe.

WHEN COUPLES STAND TOGETHER BEFORE A MIRROR THERE ARE FOUR VECTORS TO BE considered. The real and reflected relationship to each, and each's relationship to the reflection. In *Brute Force* (1947) Ted Lister (Whit Bissell) presents Cora (Ella Raines) with a fur coat. The foreground or real pair, with Lister's arm around her shoulder and Cora's face not visible, seem like an ordinary couple. The two in the mirror strike a different pose. Lister's other hand presses Cora's arm too insistently, disrupting the line of the fur. His look is harder, but at her real figure not at the reflection. Cora's gesture of folding in her own arms is resistant to Lister's embrace. She does look at his reflection and her expression is at best one of disinterest, at worst of disdain. The mirror reveals the true relationship.

N *THE BIG HEAT* (1953), MOB SOLDIER VINCE STONE (LEE MARVIN) TAKES AN ENTIRELY PROPRIETARY attitude towards his moll Debby Marsh (Gloria Grahame). In the foreground as real figures, he nuzzles against her as she leans back against him. In the mirror, his hands on her shoulders appear to pull her back, while she holds her hands non-commitally at her waist. His look is down, perhaps at her reflected face or at her body. Her lips are parted seductively yet mockingly, as her eyes seemed aimed at herself, not at Vince's image. The light from camera left that rims their hair is only visible in the mirror, which, were it not for the cluttered half table in front of it, would seem more like a doorway between two marble columns. There is an actual doorway reflected to their left and part of the opposite wall, which seems to have another mirror. This confusion of reflections and passageways makes it seem as if the characters are caught between two worlds, which will shortly become Debby's dilemma when she cooperates with Detective Bannion.

NICK ROBEY (JOHN GARFIELD) AND PEG DOBBS (SHELLEY WINTERS) ARE NOT BEFORE a mirror in *He Ran All the Way* (1951). Yet the frame and shattered glass of the window make it seem like looking into a cracked mirror. While the jagged opening frames Peg's frightened face, the edge of it slashes across Robey's visage, ominously bisecting it. For the viewer, who has likely expected from the first that the fugitive Robey will not survive, this image leaves little doubt; and moments later he perishes.

THE PLACEMENT OF THE MIRROR IN *T-MEN* (1947) CREATES AN unusual combination of subjective and objective images in one frame. The viewer can see undercover Agent Genaro (Alfred Ryder) as he faces a likely bullet. He sags against the wall and lowers his head in anticipation of the impact. At the same time, Genaro's point of view is visible in the mirror, where Moxie (Charles McGraw) holds a gun levelled at him while Genaro's partner Agent O'Brien (Dennis O'Keefe) must stand by helplessly.

CHAPTER SEVEN

NEO-NOIR

Whenever one believes that the classic period of film noir ended or what exact titles are part of that movement, no one now includes the films of the 1980s and 1990s in that grouping. Since we cannot be concerned here with how broadly commentators may define film noir in a century or two, what we perceive as new films in the noir mode, or neo-noir, add by their very imitation another perspective on the defining stylistics of the original.

Even before the first appearance of the words film noir on a contemporary one-sheet (for The Hot Spot in 1990), reviewers had already taken to labeling certain new releases as noir. Now, for any journalist, the term "noir" can stand alone and be applied to any manifestation of a dark undercurrent in American society. For those developing projects in the motion picture industry, film noir is a universally understood epithet used in thumbnail descriptions of scripts. In his recent essay on neo-noir "Kill Me Again: Movement Becomes Genre," Todd Erickson suggests that in recruiting what they perceive to be defining components of film noir to use in their movies, contemporary filmmakers have made a genre out of a movement. Since (one assumes) the term "film noir" never appeared on any original posters during the classic period, Erickson's implication is that self-awareness transforms a stylistically defined movement into an iconically defined genre. Erickson's series of interviews with new-noir filmakers for his earlier thesis had already confirmed the awareness. The new-noir films themselves can best confirm the stylistic indebtedness.

As Kathie Moffett (Jane Greer) makes a phone call under the watchful eye of strongarm man Joe Stefanos (Paul Valentine) in *Out of the Past* (1947), she appears to be completely hemmed in. Since Stefanos's boss, Whit Sterling, does not trust her, she is under constant surveillance. Just being a woman in a pool of light in a phone booth at night could easily connote isolation and danger. In the two dimensions of the frame the booth, the man, and the stairs and bricks behind her all seem to push her up against the pay phone and the stone wall on which it is mounted. The overhead source light strikes only the front of Stefanos's face and outlines a smug expression that confirms his sense of being in control. Since he stands next to a woman whose elegant hair, jewels and furs glow attractively in the overhead light, what he controls adds to his self-important pose. What Stefanos cannot see is Kathie's expression. Although her body is half-turned toward him, as if to reassure him that she has nothing to hide, her head is tilted and her face held toward the mouthpiece away from his eyes. That expression reveals a quiet determination, perhaps even confidence in being able to outwit her trench-coated guardian.

(Previous Page)

In one of the earliest neo-noir, Ryan O'Neal as the title character in *The Driver* (1977) uses a pay phone. Here the only sources is from the overhead light, so that the left and background are in total darkness, accentuating the figure's isolation. But although the booth is closed and a marble wall runs diagonally at right, the figure is in no immediate peril. The uncertain play of light behind him could be reflections off the smudged glass or someone approaching. Again the key is the character's face. While the shadows make him seem fatigued, his actions and his expression here have all suggested that he is in control, one step ahead of varied antagonists.

N *THE WINDOW* (1949), ADAPTED FROM CORNELL WOOLRICH'S *THE BOY CRIED MURDER*, Tommy (Bobby Driscoll) witnesses a murder by the couple next door; but, as Woolrich's title intimates, no one will believe him. Posed in the window through which he witnesses the crime, the railing from the fire escape creates the familiar bar motif which externalizes Tommy's feeling of helplessness and entrapment. In *The Good Son* (1993) young Mark Evans (Elijah Wood) witnesses serious misdeeds by a boy his own age. Defied by his antagonist to tell an adult who will likely not believe him, Mark receives the same visual treatment as he sits on the stairs and ponders what to do.

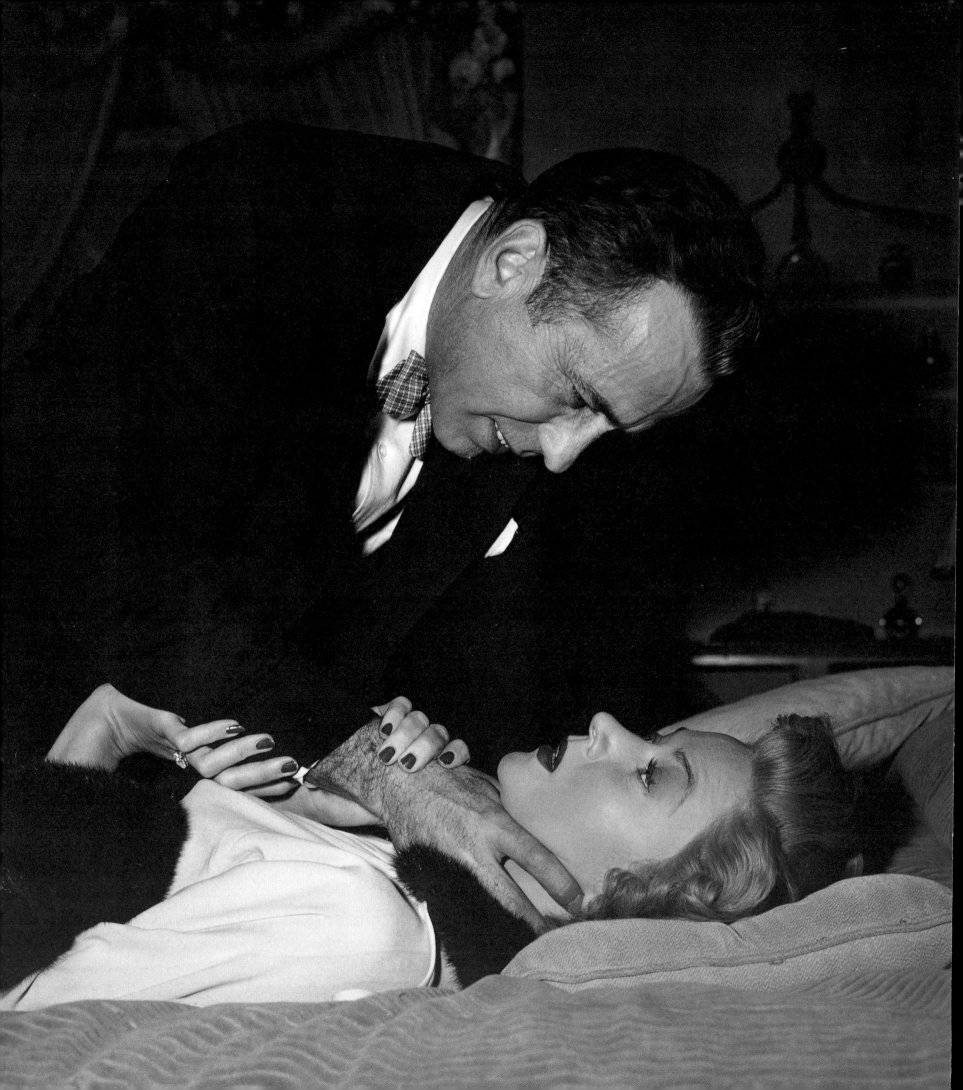

I N ADAPTING AND REFINING ELEMENTS FROM THE CLASSIC PERIOD, NEO-NOIR INHERITS THE anti-traditionalism of a movement where playing against type, breaking age restrictions, and gender reversals were rooted. When disturbed screenwriter Dixon Steele (Humphrey Bogart) attempts to control Laurel Gray (Gloria Grahame) in *In A Lonely Place* (1950), he terrorizes her, at one point pinning her to a bed and clasping his hand around her neck. The staging is direct: Laurel is terrified and Steele, veins bulging in his brow, teeth set, is out of control. When female mobster Mona Demarkov (Lena Olin) wants to control corrupt cop Jack Grimaldi (Gary Oldman) in *Romeo is Bleeding* (1993), she uses a ritual of deadly menace and sexual dominance. Handcuffed to a bed, Grimaldi cannot resist Mona's charms.

AS A GENERATION-X SLANT GAINS PROMINENCE IN NEO-NOIR, THE VERY MANNER IN WHICH characters are presented and attendant elements of style are altered to create noir variants for the 90s. The pose of Annie Laurie and Bart in the original *Gun Crazy* (1950) could be characterized in many ways, but insouciance is an unlikely adjective. Fleeing, shortly before their final, fatal confrontation with the law, the couple's desperation is obvious. Their dress, particularly the pearl necklace around Annie's neck, which is inappropriate to the wooded surroundings, is a trope for their position, the hopelessness of which can be read in their hunched postures and pained looks. Equally desperate is George Le Main (John Barrymore, Jr.) a teenager who has armed himself to confront a man who has humiliated George's father. His pinched features and awkward pose in which the rolled-up sleeve of his shirt appears to be caught in the drawer of the register where the gun was kept are typical noir indicators of his emotional intensity.

COMPARE THE POSE OF THE NEO-NOIR FUGITIVE COUPLE IN *G*UNCRAZY (1992). *D*REW *B*ARRYMORE as the troubled teenager Anita holds a much bigger gun than her father did in portraying George forty years earlier. While *Guncrazy* is not a remake (and in many ways closer to *They Live by Night* than its namesake), there are many narrative parallels with *Gun Crazy*. Despite the guns, the fast cars, and the flight from the law, the 90s couple has a different attitude, beginning with the motive, or lack of one, for their behavior. Like Bart, Howard (James Legros) is an ex-con who wants to indulge his fixation by working for a gun company. Unlike Bart, Howard has a probation officer who reins him in, perhaps explaining his glum expression as he sits in the dirt in front of his American "muscle" car. Caught up in the thrill ride, Anita never seems to grasp the seriousness of her actions, which could explain her casual attitude.

THE EVOLUTION OF NOIR INTO NEO-NOIR HAS MANY OTHER recombinant possibilities. Late in the classic period, *The Lineup* (1958) had a hit-man named Dancer (Eli Wallach) for its protagonist. Having survived by relying on the meticulous planning of his handler, Dancer is outraged at the mischance which dooms him. He kills a syndicate boss before dying in a shoot out on an unfinished freeway, a late noir twist on the dead end.

THE PROGRESSION TO DIRECTOR DON SIEGEL'S 1964 REMAKE of *The Killers* is a short one. Charlie (Lee Marvin) wears the same dark suit and tie and carries the same caliber handgun with a slightly larger silencer. But even as he dies, the laconic Charlie understands that rewards require risk and eventually everyone loses.

THE NEO-NOIR HIT MAN CAN ALSO BE A HIT WOMAN. BLENDING CHARACTERS LIKE DANCER AND Charlie with a femme fatale from the classic period creates Maggie (Bridget Fonda) in *Point of No Return* (1993, based on the French neo-noir film *La Femme Nikita*) who brings a literalness to the concept of fatal woman. Place and Peterson observed that "the noir heroines were shot in tough, unromantic close-ups of direct, undiffused light, which create a hard, statuesque surface beauty that seems more seductive but less attainable, at once alluring and impenetrable." Whether or not clasping an auto pistol to her breasts makes Maggie more alluring, the image of her, disheveled after a narrow escape and caught by a low side light against an alley wall, certainly qualifies as a neo-noir version of the unromantic close-up. The whiteness of the skin with beads of water on her shoulder at the shadow line and the unruly strands of hair framing the penetrating blue eyes create a visual center of deadly beauty. Her finger on the trigger of the potent and phallic weapon completes the fusion of hit man/woman.

I N SOME INSTANCES FILM NOIR COULD BECOME STYLE FOR STYLE'S SAKE, and neo-noir has inherited this tendency. This shot from *Criminal Court* (1946) flaunts the trappings of the noir style: a key light up high and behind reveals two prototypical figures, one in pin stripes (Tom Conway, a lawyer), one in an immaculate trenchcoat (a shamus), both with their hats on inside and smoking unfiltered cigarettes. But nothing can compare to the shadow pattern thrown by the fill light on the back wall. Dark lines criss cross two, three, perhaps four times, until a dizzying vortex is formed at the center of the frame behind the two men.

FOR A NEO-NOIR EXAMPLE OF THOSE SHADOW PATTERNS, THE ENDING OF *The Last Boy Scout* (1991) features a disaffected, substance abusing P.I. Joe Hallenbeck (Bruce Willis) taking a stand against the bad guys at a football stadium. While being shot at from above and below and menaced by a helicopter overhead, he holds his ground on a steel walkway as light streams through from below. To a certain extent, the visual confusion of the lighting is appropriate to an action scene; but when the action creates its own confusion, embellishment of this sort distracts and defocuses the viewer.

THE PLAYER IS ONE OF WRITER/DIRECTOR WALTER HILL'S SELF-CONSCIOUS NOIR ARCHETYPES in *The Driver*. Inspired as much by Jean Pierre Melville's *Le Samourai* (1967) as by classic American film noir, none of *The Driver*'s characters have names and, like the anonymous female gambler portrayed by Isabelle Adjani, find widely variant antecedents in the classic period. Like all of *The Driver*'s characters, the Player dresses in black; but Adjani's accent as well as her shoulder-length hair, arched brow, and high cheekbones lend the character the exotic appeal of a traditional femme fatale à la Rita Hayworth in *Gilda*. At the same time, her clipped speech and other mannerisms could also recall the gambling Baroness (Suzanne Flon, above) in *Mr. Arkadin* (1955).

THE OVERSIZED CLOCK IN FRONT OF WHICH RITA JOHNSON AND RAY MILLAND WERE posed for *The Big Clock* (1948) is not in the movie but merely a prop for a publicity shot. Still its symbolic affect could easily be incorporated into a film in the neo-noir era. In *Rumble Fish* (1983), Patterson the Cop (William Smith) confronts Rusty-James (Matt Dillon, center) and his brother, the Motorcycle Boy (Mickey Rourke) by the side of a truck transporting a huge clock face.

A S A GENRE, NEO-NOIR CAN INVOKE EXPECTATIONS IN THE VIEWER. WHEN HE WROTE ABOUT "the power of light and what it can do to the mind of the audience," John Alton was referring to a broader range of expectations that filter how a spectator reads any scene through its assembled physical characteristics. By the end of the classic period, with or without a cognizance of the term "film noir," audiences already had a refined set of expectations derived from their experience of collectively viewing the body of films that constituted the noir cycle. As a consequence, anyone observing the phenomena of film noir as movement or cycle and neo-noir as genre today could derive almost identical expectations in terms of both narrative content and style. In the classic period, style based on manipulation eventually became part of expectation based on reiteration.

In the period drama, *Murder in the First* (1994), Christian Slater (left) and Kevin Bacon portray attorney and condemned client. As with so many film noir the motif imposes a stylistic filter on the action. The prisoner's embryonic pose reveals his mental state while the direct light reveals the scarred face as dark foreground bars fracture the frame. The attorney, while physically closer to his client, is more distant from the viewer and behind another set of bars. In the darkness beyond he is visible only from the waist up, one eye obliterated behind a bar. The staging compliments the drama without significantly redirecting the viewer's perception of the figures in the frame but reinforcing the sense of isolation from each other and from the spectator.

N *The Silence of the Lambs* (1991) the stylistic overlay is more telling. As Clarice Starling (Jodie Foster) visits psychopathic killer Hannibal Lecter (Anthony Hopkins) in a high security mental ward, she must communicate with him through a glass partition. By placing the camera inside the glass, the spectator is figuratively inside Lecter's cell. More significantly it permits a reflection on Lecter to be visible on the inside of the glass. The shot is not from his point of view, so Starling looks to her right and not directly at the camera. The spectral reflection is out of focus but it is clear that in the two dimensions of the frame, Lecter's cheek overlays Starling's hair. Already uneasy knowing Lecter's history of chilling violence, Starling cannot completely conceal her fear. On her lapel, the badge marked "Visitor Pass" hangs like a totem against the evil, for it means that Starling can leave at any time and never come face-to-face with Lecter again. While the undiffused light from slightly above and to her left flares out across her cheek and brow masking most of the detail in the skin, the slight sag of her shoulders, the apprehensive lean forward at the waist, communicate the mesmeric experience of being in Lecter's presence. And the figurative brush against his cheek causes an involuntary shudder. In its simplicity this visual trope helps to balance the literal horrors that are to be seen in *The Silence of the Lambs*.

In the best of film noir, style works to expand the spectator's reading of the physical reality and the surface drama. The noir style can take a multiplicity of character viewpoints and render the relationship between them. It can create a pictorial equivalent of the emotional reality. As John Alton observed, "people . . . illuminated by light, in life or in pictures, produce psychological impressions." For all its complex workings with the expectations and perceptions of the spectator, as it developed over two decades, nothing in the noir style deviated from this fundamental principal. And as it survives today, in the homages and reconstructions of the noir mood by a new generation of filmmakers, the same is still true.

VISITOR
PASS

Baltimore State Forensic Hospital

Index of Names and Film Titles